D1602830

COURT-MARTIAL OF APACHE KID

COURT-MARTIAL OF APACHE KID

The Renegade of Renegades

CLARE V. MCKANNA, JR.

FOREWORD BY SIDNEY L. HARRING

TEXAS TECH UNIVERSITY PRESS

Book design by Mark McGarry, Texas Type & Book Works.

Library of Congress Cataloging-in-Publication Data
McKanna, Clare V. (Clare Vernon), 1935–
Court-martial of Apache Kid, the renegade of renegades /
Clare V. McKanna, Jr. ; foreword by Sidney L. Harring.
p. cm.
Includes bibliographical references and index.
Summary: "Traces the 1887 legal odyssey of First Sergeant Kid,
an Apache scout charged with desertion and mutiny. Details Kid's trials by
three Arizona Territory legal systems—Apache, military, and civilian—and explores
the development of military law along with Kid's transition from scout to
legendary renegade"—Provided by publisher.
ISBN 978-0-89672-652-9 (hardcover : alk. paper)
1. Apache Kid, b. ca 1860. 2. Apache Kid, b. ca 1860—Trials, litigation, etc.
3. Apache Indians—Arizona—Biography. 4. Indian scouts—Arizona—
Biography. 5. Indian outlaws—Arizona—Biography. 6. Trials (Military offenses)—
United States—History—19th century. I. Title.
E99.A6A5956 2009
979.1004'97—dc22
[B]
2009008730

Printed in the United States of America
09 10 11 12 13 14 15 16 17 / 9 8 7 6 5 4 3 2 1

Texas Tech University Press
Box 41037
Lubbock, Texas 79409–1037 USA
800.832.4042
ttup@ttu.edu
www.ttup.ttu.edu

For
Roger Cunniff
scholar, critic, good friend,
a true Renaissance man

CONTENTS

ILLUSTRATIONS

MAPS

FOREWORD

Over the past twenty years a new Indian history has substantially rewritten the history of the European conquest of the Americas. In this remarkable book, Clare McKanna adds to this canon with an insightful, well written, and modestly understated classic story, that of Apache Kid, a "renegade" who was never caught, retold as legal history.

Native people met European conquest in a wide variety of ways, best understood through the tools of ethnohistory, trying to imagine Indian thinking at the time and extrapolating that thought into their action, with careful attention to documenting the known historical context. This is a demanding task for any historian, for there is always a tendency to substitute the historian's thinking for that of long dead Indian warriors. McKanna is very deliberate in his analysis and always either lets the almost unknown Apache Kid speak for himself or lets the reader's imagination fill in the blank parts.

"Almost unknown" probably describes every Indian actor of the nineteenth century, but Apache Kid remains at the extreme end of this description, for we do not, for certain, even know his real name. And his story involves a stereotyped model of "living between two worlds" for only six years in the 1880s before being twice tried, being initially sentenced to death by a court-martial, having that sentence commuted to a prison sentence, then being retried in a civilian court and escaping to roam the mountains of the border country between Arizona and Mexico, never caught, with no record at all of his fate. In the iconic histories of Indians of this period he roams the same borderlands as Geronimo, but he escapes Geronimo's fate of capture, exile to prison in Florida and to Fort Sill, Oklahoma, and then a sad, captive death more than thirty years after so valiantly fighting for the freedom of his people.

While the full story of the Apache and Indian wars still must be written, the model of Indian warfare as a response to the European conquest reads like high adventure and even poetry (as in Chief Joseph's famous surrender statement, "From where the sun now stands, I will fight no more forever") and makes perfect sense historically. Given as many Indian wars as there were, these wars were still not the way most Indians came to terms with the loss of their lands, their sovereignty, and their cultures. Most Indian peoples tried to accommodate white aggression peacefully. If we know too little about the ethnohistory of the Indian wars, we know even less about Native accommodation to white America.

There are any number of ways this can be studied, but one of them clearly is legal history, for, as de Tocqueville wrote, "while the Spanish came with dogs, the Americans came with laws, and the result was tragically the same." The United States, perhaps uniquely in the world, tried to impose legal order on its frontier, including Indian peoples, then sovereign in their own land. The result of this is thousands of legal events, many of them criminal trials, with records left in archives throughout the country. Some of these cases led to Indian victories. For example, Crow Dog, a Brulé Sioux contemporary of Apache Kid, had his murder conviction and death sentence reversed by the U.S. Supreme Court in 1883 and returned to a simple cabin at the farthest corner of the reservation, where he remained for over thirty years, encouraging his people to continue to resist in any way possible and reminding them that American law was weak and ineffective. Apache Kid faced both military and territorial legal systems that did him great injustice, repeatedly convicting him of crimes that he was probably not guilty of. And he lived in a third legal system, that of traditional Apache law, giving rise to the events that put him in conflict with the two American legal systems. In the context of the injustice that he faced, escape was probably the only way out for Apache Kid. This is another story of the failure of law to do justice in complicated political and intercultural situations, surely not unfamiliar in the world today.

Kid, born about 1859 or 1860 near what would become the San Carlos Agency, was the grandson of a chief, Togodechuz. While he would ultimately be known as a "San Carlos" Apache, the Apaches were organized into closeknit bands, and it was the government that forced many of these different bands to live together at the agency. Apache Kid came of age during the various "Apache Wars" that tore Arizona apart in the 1870s and 1880s, ending with the capture of Geronimo in 1886. As a young man Kid would have been toughened and trained to be a warrior: running long distances, living off the desert, bathing in ice cold water, and hunting game. By all accounts he was an expert horseman. He would have been raised in traditional Apache culture and religion.

In June 1882 Apache Kid enlisted as a scout with the Tenth Cavalry of the U.S. Army at Fort Apache, changing his life forever and setting the stage for the "Apache Kid" legend. How, at the age of about twenty-two, he made this decision, or what the meaning of it was, can never be known, because Kid left no account of most of his actions. Telling this story is the task that McKanna faces, and he tells it brilliantly.

This clearly is one of the most classic "between two worlds" stories that can be told, and in turn it is one story of how Indian America came under United States control—how the Indian nations were dominated by means of law, culture, religion, and politics. We do not know enough about any of these stories—and there are hundreds of them in the litera-ture—and the Apache chiefs who chose not to fight but somehow to accommodate American power, white settlement, and relocation to reservations.

Within a month of his enlistment Apache Kid did great service to the U.S. Army against other Apaches at the Battle of Big Dry Wash. He con-tinued in the army, enlisting as needed, and fought in the Apache Wars until the capture of Geronimo in 1886 and Kid's court-martial in 1888. Apache Kid was court-martialed for mutiny and desertion for abandon-ing his post and hunting down and killing an Apache in revenge for killing his grandfather. This killing would have occurred under tradi-tional Apache law and indicates that Kid was, in fact, living in both worlds and carried out this execution, clearly risking his own life and place among the army scouts, because he was still an Apache, operating within traditional cultural boundaries.

We know essentially nothing of his motivation. But this is the task of the historian, to reconstitute as much of this story with as much integrity as can be managed. Some historians, too eager to tell a good story and unwilling to acknowledge how much they do not know, over-interpret these histories, reading far too much into a few statements or actions. But McKanna does not. Masterfully, he has constructed the story from what he does know. He is a good historian and has done yeoman's work with the primary sources. He has set the stage of the Apache Wars as well as of the frontier U.S. Army.

Perhaps most interesting, after the Kid's story itself, is McKanna's careful and detailed analysis of military law. In the context of the current controversy over the imprisonment and military trials of "unlawful combatants" from Iraq and Afghanistan, this legal history is important and raises a number of questions about the relationship between these proceedings and native peoples. Whatever the necessity of military law to govern a functioning army, its application to Indians was always tenuous—arguably a complete fiction, as it is not clear that Apache Kid, or any of the Indian scouts, were ever trained in this law or even had any knowledge of it, as regular soldiers would have. This conceit, that Indians enlisted as scouts were under military law, was convenient in frontier Arizona precisely because the army would have known full well that the line between a settled Apache and an Apache at war was also a fiction.

The Apache, as probably did all other Indians, faced very difficult choices in attempting to accommodate American invasion of their lands. The time from first settler contact to the reservation era was longer than most historians formerly thought, because the Indians had experienced some knowledge of whites since the 1600s, earlier in the Southwest, but the displacement of most tribes by white settlers happened in a few generations, when settlement finally arrived. It was only after the Civil War that large numbers of white settlers came to Arizona, and the Apache Wars were over in less than twenty years—the short lifetime of a twenty-two-year-old Apache army scout.

While we might easily imagine clear motivation for Indian wars, relatively speaking, we know much less about the Indians that chose to accommodate. One hypothesis is that these Indians believed that they could effectively protect their cultural identities, sovereignty, and economic livelihoods by co-opting white institutions. Indeed, they had some real advantages that might help them do so. They had strong cultures, effective leadership structures, their own languages, and, even on a reservation, most of the territory beyond the Indian agent's house and buildings. The literature is replete with stories of Indians' incorporating the shell of western religion around their own religious beliefs, using hunting trips to instill a warrior culture in the young and American holidays, including the Fourth of July, to celebrate their own religious or cultural ceremonials.

In this context there cannot be much question that Indian warriors used white military or paramilitary organizations to carry on their warrior cultures. The literature of the Indian police clearly shows that agency police structures reflected traditional tribal structures, often incorporating traditional chiefs into the command structure. Indian police received military training, were issued guns, and rode horses. Therefore, when Apache Kid enlists in the U.S. Army it is not difficult to imagine that many of the elements of this task are directly incorporated from Apache culture. Indeed, the Apache scouts lived together in traditional wickiups, the wooden frame dwelling structures in which they grew up. They would have spent most of their days together, speaking their Apache language.

McKanna describes this day-to-day life in great detail. Being a scout was a part-time job. Army scouts were enlisted for campaigns, then dismissed when the campaign was over, then re-recruited for the next campaign. Kid, between 1882 and 1888, spent only about six months a year as a scout, returning to his people the other half of the time. Thus, when

Kid suddenly leaves the fort to kill the man who killed his grandfather, this is a much less abrupt break from his role as a scout than it might seem; he was already spending half of each year in his band, where he was in the role of grandson of a chief, the man who had taught him how to become a warrior.

When Apache Kid kills Rip, the man who had killed his grandfather, it is, following from the above, not such a clearly defined departure from his role as an Army scout. It is doubtful that, at the time, Kid even felt that he was "between two laws." His sense of his traditional law would have been strong. It is not clear that he had an equivalent sense of his place under military or territorial law. While he might have expected some official military response to his "offense"—being away without leave for five days—this would have been a trivial offense within his context. To be convicted, sentenced to death, and then sent to Alcatraz would have been an unbelievable result, one that must have weighed on Kid with great force.

But Apache Kid was, probably unknowingly, caught up in another system of laws. As the Apache Wars continued into the 1880s, Arizona Territory had another set of courts, both federal and territorial. When Apache warriors left their reservations and killed white settlers, these acts could be considered "acts of war," but they could also be interpreted by local authorities, responsive to their settler constituencies, as simple acts of murder, arson, or robbery. Instead of treating such warriors as military prisoners and sending them east, as with Geronimo and his band, they could convict them of serious crimes and send them to the gallows or to rot in the territorial prison at Yuma. This was to be the fate of Kid and the warriors he rode with—and only Kid escaped it.

The last chapter of this story is perhaps the most important. Of all the modes of Indian adaptation to the onslaught of American settlement, the role of the renegade is that least written about. Legal history is about the power of law as a social force. As such it must include both the history of those within the reach of law—and also the history of those beyond the reach of law. Any Indian warrior stuck on a reservation has to have known that he could simply take his horse and gun and leave. If the "outlaw" is part of western legal culture, then it has to be clear that Indians had the same choice to go that route as whites did. In this sense the Kid is probably typical: he spent at least six years in his early twenties, in the changing environment of 1880s Arizona, trying to find a place for himself as a young male Apache. When he finally was released from a chain gang, there truly was no going back. His choice was either to live the rest of his life as an outlaw or to die in a dingy cell in the territorial prison. So he became the best known renegade Indian in American history—and the most successful, because he was never caught. This is another classic adaptation story that must apply to untold thousands of other Indians "caught between two worlds." We are indebted to Clare McKanna for taking us so far with this story. We can only hope that others take up this challenge and record more of this history.

SIDNEY L. HARRING
City University of New York

PREFACE

In May 1887 Apache Kid left his duty station as first sergeant of scouts at San Carlos Agency and, with fellow band members, rode south to Aravaipa Canyon, where he killed Rip, a member of a rival band, in retribution for the murder of his grandfather six months earlier. At a court-martial Kid was charged with desertion and mutiny, convicted, and incarcerated in Alcatraz. Kid became caught up in a vortex that included three legal systems: Apache, military, and civil. During the nineteenth century military law was fraught with dissension and change; this study will allow us to gain insights into how the military legal system developed on the frontier. Although other Apache defendants also suffered injustice in the Arizona Territory under the heavy-handed legal systems, both civil and military, Kid was chosen as the focus of this study because of his fame and the availability of a court-martial transcript. Unlike Geronimo, who was captured and imprisoned, Kid escaped from the custody of the Gila County sheriff while being transported to the Arizona Territorial Prison in Yuma and became a renegade. There is no black-and-white history about Kid; instead, we have many shades of gray that make it difficult to paint an accurate portrait of his character and life. During his court-martial Kid spoke only seven hundred words. Still, what we do have offers us a chance to gain some impressions about him. Although we are unsure of his Apache name, birth date, or parents, records concerning his court-martial in 1887 offer us an opportunity to examine and discover something of value about Apache Kid and what he represented as a legendary figure in Arizona.

ACKNOWLEDGMENTS

I owe a great debt of gratitude to Professor Emeritus Roger Cunniff, Department of History, San Diego State University, who has been my alter ego, critic, and good friend. Roger's superb organizational and editorial skills and his ability to see the trees for the forest were instrumental in developing and completing this book. I also need to thank Professor Clare Colquitt, Department of Comparative Literature and English, San Diego State University, for her critical reading. Clare is a good friend and honest critic who provided advice on how to improve the narrative. Judith Keeling, editor-in-chief, Texas Tech University Press, provided moral support throughout the review process, and I also wish to thank the two anonymous reviewers and the editorial board members who offered much-needed criticism that helped to shape the final manuscript.

I give special thanks to Melodie Tune, graphic artist, Instructional Technology Services, San Diego State University, for designing and completing the maps for this book. I would like to acknowledge archivists Wendi Goen and Nancy Sawyer at the Arizona State Archives, Phoenix, who provided invaluable assistance in locating court records and photographs. The archivists of the Old Military Records, National Archives, also provided much-needed help by locating and copying the Apache Kid court-martial file. Finally, special thanks go to the College of Arts and Letters, San Diego State University, for funding my exploratory research in the summer of 2000.

COURT-MARTIAL OF APACHE KID

To know the truth of history is to realize its ultimate myth and its inevitable ambiguity.

ROY P. BASLER

PROLOGUE

APACHE KID

The beginnings and end of the Apache Kid are shrouded in mystery. Only in the prime of his spectacular life does he stand highlighted on the horizon of southwestern history.

DAN THRAPP, *Al Sieber,* 320

.　.　.

On Friday morning, November 1, 1889, Gila County Sheriff Glen Reynolds, Deputy W. A. Holmes, and stagecoach driver Eugene Middleton were transporting to the Arizona Territorial Prison in Yuma eight Apaches recently convicted of various crimes by Gila County authorities. The most notorious among them was the young Apache scout known as Kid. Al Sieber had offered to provide an Apache scout escort, but Reynolds allegedly said: "I do not need your scouts, I can take those Indians alone with a corn-cob and a lightning-bug."[1] Reynolds may have underestimated the desperate nature of his Apache prisoners, some of whom probably felt betrayed by both military and Gila County court officials.

Sheriff Reynolds planned to escort his prisoners southwest from Globe to Riverside on the San Pedro River, a distance of about thirty miles, then turn westward twenty-five miles to Florence and finally twenty miles further on to Casa Grande, where he would place the prisoners on a train

bound for Yuma. As planned, they stopped overnight at Riverside, and
very early Saturday morning the prisoners were loaded into the stagecoach, which followed a road along the Gila River as they headed
towards Florence. This was rather rugged country with small hills on
both sides of the river, and the stagecoach had to ascend several grades
along this road, the first about four miles from Riverside. As they began
to climb the grade, Sheriff Reynolds ordered six of the Apache prisoners to get out of the stagecoach and walk behind. To allow them to
walk, the lawmen removed the shackles from their legs and handcuffed
them in pairs. Kid and Hoscalte remained handcuffed and shackled
inside the stagecoach. Sheriff Reynolds walked carelessly behind the
stagecoach with Jesús Avott, a Hispanic prisoner, and the Apache prisoners followed behind, while Deputy Holmes brought up the rear. It
was still dark and, since it was a very cold morning, both the sheriff and
his deputy were wearing heavy overcoats and gloves. Suddenly, the
Apache prisoners let out a yell, began to grapple with Reynolds and
Holmes, and were able to seize a rifle and a shotgun. Although
Bachoandoth shot the sheriff, he did not shoot the deputy down;
apparently, Holmes died of a heart attack. During the struggle between
Reynolds and the Apache prisoners the sheriff was unable to reach his
revolver because his buttoned overcoat covered his six-gun. Sayes later
testified that Bachoandoth, also known as Pashtentah, was the prisoner
who shot the sheriff with a rifle, and soon afterward Reynolds received
a fatal charge of buckshot from his own gun through the head. After
they had killed Reynolds the Apache prisoners used the keys to the
handcuffs and manacles to free Kid and Hoscalte, who were still locked
up in the stagecoach.[2]

When Middleton, the stagecoach driver, heard the shots he stopped
the horses, looked back, and received a bullet in his right cheek.
Middleton fell from the stagecoach and feigned death. As the driver lay
wounded on the ground, Kid, apparently knowing that he was still alive,
stopped Elcahn from attacking him with a rock, but the Apache prisoners stripped off his coat and rifled his pockets searching for money. After

shooting the sheriff, Bachoandoth examined the sheriff's pockets and took his gold watch and two hundred dollars in cash. The Apache prisoners escaped with three six-shooters, a rifle, and a shotgun. Jesús Avott fled for his life and was not chased by the Apache prisoners, who quickly made their escape into the barren desert landscape. Avott walked to Florence to alert the sheriff of Pinal County, while the wounded Middleton returned to Riverside to seek medical attention and give the alarm.[3]

In Florence soon after the killings, Pinal County Sheriff Jerry Fryer quickly raised and led a posse in pursuit, with Justice J. B. Fitch, Dr. A. S. Adler, and a coroner's jury following to hold an autopsy at the crime scene. The posse tracked the fugitives across the San Pedro River near Zellweger's ranch and continued on over mountains and across the inhospitable desert. Occasionally they found discarded items belonging to the dead men.[4] After the escape, a telegram reached Captain John L. Bullis at San Carlos, who alerted military authorities at Fort Thomas and other military posts. By 3:00 p.m. the U.S. Cavalry, with Apache scouts, quickly began to follow the trail of the fugitives, and within a few hours several other military units were involved in the chase. The Pinal County posse discovered the carcass of a steer that had been killed for food. When the exhausted posse came across troops following the trail, they gave up the chase and returned to Florence. Military units pursued the fugitives into the foothills of the Saddle Mountains at the northern end of Aravaipa Canyon, where rain and snow washed out the trail. This region, which included Ash Creek and Lookout Mountain, was in the southern portion of San Carlos and was well known to Kid, who had grown up near there. Unconfirmed rumors suggested that Kid and Bachoandoth may have been seen the next day on the San Carlos River near the agency.[5]

Various conflicting newspaper accounts created confusion about exactly what had happened during the escape. For example, one reporter claimed that Hoscalte had wrenched Holmes's gun out of his hands while the others grappled with Reynolds. Later, Sayes testified that he and Bachoandoth grabbed Reynolds and that Sayes pinned his arms while Bachoandoth, after taking Holmes's gun, shot Reynolds in the left shoulder. Avott and Sayes both claimed that Hoscalte remained shackled in the stagecoach with Kid and did not take part in the killings. According to Avott's testimony, two others, Hastindutoday and Bithejabetishtocean, also did not participate in the attack on the sheriff and his deputy. Newspapers reported that Holmes had been shot, but the autopsy revealed no wounds; the coroner's jury ruled that he had died of a heart attack. Capturing these desperate fugitives became a daunting task that continued for months. However, in July 1890 Josh and several other Indian scouts apparently gained the confidence of one fugitive, killed him, cut off his head, and returned with it to San Carlos. The man who lost his head was Bachoandoth. By mid-1890, five of the original eight Apache convicts were believed to be dead. Pursuers trailed and captured Sayes on July 25.[6]

On August 3, 1890, a *New York Times* editorial reported that "Kid's gang" was being broken up by the U.S. Cavalry and Apache scouts. To call the fugitives "Kid's gang" may be a misnomer; it is likely that he quickly separated from them or he would have been caught as well.[7] By the end of 1890, only Kid remained free: he would become an Arizona legend.

Exactly who was Apache Kid, and why did he gain such notoriety? Anyone who chooses to examine historically the life of this fascinating Apache faces a daunting task. Kid left neither letters nor documents that might provide us with some idea about how he viewed his world overrun by an alien society that incorporated an intense hatred for Apaches into its social and legal systems. Apache oral narratives discussing Kid were selected to help provide a little more complexity in our cultural search for the Indian perspective. It should be understood, however, that these were composed after the events we examine here. Although they reflect the myths surrounding Kid and his exploits, they nevertheless provide

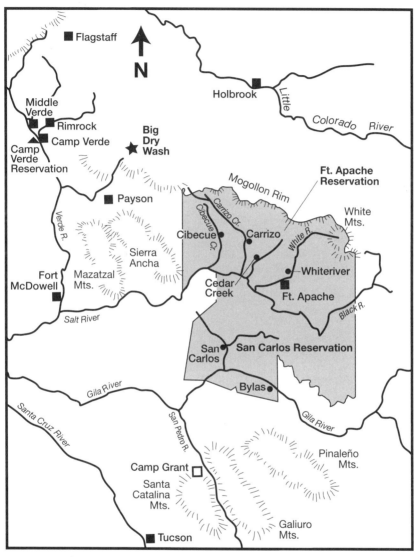

Nineteenth-century Arizona, showing San Carlos Reservation. Courtesy Melodie Tune, graphic artist, Instructional Technology Services, San Diego State University

an important Apache perspective. The secondary literature on Kid, for the most part untrustworthy and superficial, is of very little help and is used only sparingly and with caution. This leaves us with a body of material that has the virtue of being primary and contemporary with events but that is exclusively white-generated. This includes the court-martial transcript, government and military documents, civilian and military correspondence, the reports of the San Carlos Indian agents, and newspapers.

Because we know so little about Kid, his court-martial in 1887 offers some enticing possibilities that need to be explored. What is most striking about the trial transcript is the paucity of real information about Kid. His testimony amounted to just seven hundred words that reveal little about who he really was. Despite this, Kid's court-martial provides some intriguing historical clues about him and also illuminates the military justice system and its strengths and weaknesses in dealing with Native Americans who served as scouts. One must admit that no matter what is revealed by examining his court-martial, Kid will remain an enigma. How did Kid move so quickly from virtual obscurity into the limelight during the late nineteenth century? What conditions at San Carlos Agency in the Arizona Territory could create this Apache scout who incited the passions of whites and gained allegiance from Apaches? Why did he continue to raid San Carlos for women, and why was he so skilled at eluding the well-equipped military and civilian pursuers?

As if to increase the mystery, Kid's true Apache name remains unknown. The U.S. Army records listed this remarkable scout as Kid, with no other designation. Sayes, a member of Kid's band, claimed that his Indian name was Shisininty. It might seem logical that a fellow band member would know his real name, but there are many other intriguing possibilities. For example, during Kid's court-martial Tony, an Indian scout, when asked if he knew Kid's real name, replied, "His Indian name is Hahouantell, white men call him Kid."[8] And various writers have provided numerous versions of his Apache name that include Eskibinadel, Gonteee, Haskaybaynayntal, Ohyessonna, Oskabennantelz, Skibenanted, and Zenogolache. However, Kid's legitimate Apache name remains a mystery. Kid did not receive the added nickname "Apache" until he became a renegade. Since the settlers hated the Apaches, no doubt it provided a way to label him as being especially infamous and dangerous. It seems odd that we know the Apache names of Geronimo, Nana, Ulzana, and many others but not Kid's true name. By the end of the nineteenth century he had been reduced to an epithet applied by white society; thus, Kid comes to stand not for a real person but for a composite of all renegade Apaches, a symbol of the "other." Geronimo was a specific person who could be hunted down and exiled to a prison in Florida; however, this composite "Apache Kid" became a cultural icon, an indigenous symbol of a shifting historical reality.

Apache Kid, 1880s. Courtesy Arizona State Library, Archives and Public Records, History and Archives Division, Phoenix, #95-9002

The origins of Kid are sketchy. His exact birth date is unknown, but government documents listing his tours of duty as a scout suggest that he was born about 1859 or 1860. Kid was about eleven years old when General George Crook conducted his famous 1871–72 campaign against the White Mountain Apaches along the Mogollon Rim country from Prescott to Fort Apache. These and similar campaigns against Apaches continued periodically until Geronimo finally surrendered in 1886. Kid and many other Apaches were born and raised during a turbulent era, a period of troubled times at San Carlos Agency with the normal lifestyle of the Apaches under direct assault by whites who wanted their land and resources. Any Apache child raised during this period would have experienced difficulty in adjusting to this system.

Kid was born in Aravaipa Canyon about twenty-five miles south of San Carlos. Although we have no documents that reveal his childhood, we can assume that, like other young Apache boys during the 1860s, he received an amulet for good luck. Such a fetish might be an arrow point or some other charm worn around the neck on a cord to ward off lightning or sickness. It was believed to bring good luck, and many Apache scouts wore them while on the trail of Geronimo and other Apaches. At least one photograph, taken between 1887 and 1889, shows Kid wearing one that is long and slender. Physical as well as spiritual well-being was important to Apaches. At age eight to ten boys were forced to become physically toughened by getting up before dawn and swimming in a nearby stream. These bathing exercises continued year around, and in the winter the boys sometimes had to break the thin ice and plunge into ice cold water. When they had finished their swim they were ordered by elder men to run slowly up to the top of the nearest hill or small mountain and then race back to determine who was the swiftest runner. Kid apparently became very proficient at running long distance at a very rapid pace and displayed great stamina while on scouting expeditions. At the court-martial Gonshayee testified that during the mutiny Kid had quickly fled San Carlos on foot and claimed: "He is better than a horse, can run better than a horse."[9] It may be exaggeration, but the chief's testimony indicates that Kid developed important skills as a youth and was physically robust. This early regimen of physical exercise would later enable him to raid San Carlos, capture women, and miraculously elude his military pursuers and disappear unmolested into the Sierra Madre of Mexico.

During these childhood rituals Apache boys were sometimes required to run with a mouthful of water to train them to breathe through the nose. Other toughening included carrying a rock in each hand to increase their stamina. John Rope, an Apache scout, remembered that when he was about eight years old he first began to swim and run early in the morning. Rope's father explained that he needed to develop these skills at a young age to learn to elude any wild animals that might attack him, such as bears or mountain lions. The boys were often trained by an elder, such as a grandfather, who took responsibility for making sure that they did their early morning swim and run. The elders would sometimes run with them to push them to their endurance. In such a harsh environment this physical toughening was essential to make them self-reliant and able to defend themselves.[10]

Young Apache boys were required to know the names of plants, trees, and birds and how to identify plants that were edible and the cactus that would provide fruit and water as well. They also learned to identify and follow the tracks of deer, bear, coyotes, and other animals. At age seven or eight the boys usually received their first bow and quiver of arrows from an elder such as a maternal grandfather. They were trained in their use and encouraged to practice regularly so that they could learn how to kill birds and small animals. By age twelve they had developed sufficient skills to kill rabbits, squirrels, quail, and wood rats, which could be used as food. Later, at age fifteen, young boys were taken out deer hunting, a much more serious endeavor because it would help feed the entire family. It is likely that Togodechuz, Kid's grandfather, accompanied the young hunter to show him how to track and kill a deer. John Rope remembered that he learned by watching others hunt, skin, and butcher their game. He recalled being fifteen when he skinned and butchered his first deer.[11] Kid and other boys were instructed always to keep alert while hunting and remain in good shape, because their training was aimed at enabling them to accompany raiding parties when they matured.

It was common for young Apaches to learn certain rituals designed to improve their chances of success in hunting and killing deer. Sometimes they would put antlers from a previous kill in a tree as an offering. The deer was one of the most important game animals, and young boys were required to maintain certain traditions before the hunt. They usually fasted and took sweat baths to eliminate odors that might alert the deer being stalked. Any appearance of ravens or crows before a hunt was an omen that it would be a good day to hunt deer. Both those birds tended to hang around during a hunt to gain access to the remains of the kill. The hunters also might set aside a portion of the internal organs to make a good luck offering to *gaagé*—the raven.[12] These clever birds usually watched and followed a hunter looking for deer. They had extraordinary eyesight and seemed to know where the deer were. The most intense hunting occurred during the fall, when the deer were the fattest. Deer were normally killed with bows and arrows, but later rifles were commonly used.[13]

Encouraged to ride horses at about three or four years of age, young boys were put up on a burro or a gentle horse and watched carefully. It was considered to be essential that they learn to handle horses early to assure that they would develop equestrian skills essential to any young Apache trying to survive in the desert. By age ten boys were required to help the family take care of their horses. They were usually sent out early in the morning to drive the horses from their grazing area back to the camp and were required to water their horses three times a day. By the time Kid was about thirteen he was expected to be an expert rider; his years of scouting indicate that he had meticulously perfected his skills handling horses.[14]

Apache boys tended to be lean, agile, wiry, quick, and endowed with physical endurance, qualities highly prized by their elders. Photographs reveal that Kid, listed in military records at five feet nine inches tall, was slender and well built. Apache boys were encouraged to keep their bodies clean and to use their best clothes for any spiritual ceremonies performed by their tribal bands. Young boys respected their elders and emulated their behavior. For example, one young Apache boy of eight observed his maternal uncle returning from a scout enlistment and decided that he would like to be a scout someday. For most Apaches "the two highest attainments for a man were to become a powerful and influential shaman or a great hunter, warrior, and leader."[15]

Kid displayed remarkable leadership qualities and became a superb first sergeant of scouts. In general, the ability and personal magnetism of the leader determines his effectiveness within the band. Normally, when a band chief died, one of his sons would be the first choice to replace him. It is believed that Kid's father was no longer living at this time, so Kid could have succeeded his grandfather, Togodechuz, as band chief but chose not to do so. Kid may have felt some conflict between his Apache band duties and his position with the U.S. Army as a scout. Could he have held both positions? It is possible that his shifting lifestyle had caused confusion about his loyalties to both. Could Kid be a scout first and an Apache second? Despite his considerable influence, his status as a scout may have caused him to refuse the position as band chief.

During the nineteenth century the federal government tried to identify Apache band members by assigning letters and numbers to each married man, who was required to wear around his neck a small metal tag inscribed with a number. Because Apache names were difficult to pronounce and spell, white authorities believed this system to be the solution to the problem of identification. These tags also made it easier to develop census rolls at San Carlos and Fort Apache. Each member of the band received a similar tag with a specific number. Grenville Goodwin notes that each tag band had a chief selected and recognized by the government, who always received the number 1.[16] For example, Gonshayee, chief of his Aravaipa band, received a tag labeled SI-1. These letter designations were developed by the governmental authorities, but they held no significance to the Apaches prior to the establishment of this numbering system.

Most sources agree that Kid married one of the daughters of SL band chief Eskiminzin, possibly named Nahthledeztelth, with whom he grew up in Aravaipa Canyon. Eskiminzin had considerable influence at San Carlos, garnered by assisting the U.S. Army; consequently, by marrying his daughter Kid increased his social status and importance among the Aravaipa Apaches. When a daughter married, she and her husband would usually live near her parents. This strengthened the bond between the two families; such strong ties between marriage connections, status, and leadership were important within Apache society.[17] That may help to explain why Kid was offered the chief's position upon the death of his grandfather, the former SI band chief. Normally a chief would exhibit leadership, take charge, and deal with issues confronting the band. Kid possessed these qualities.

Kid's connections with Al Sieber, chief of scouts, a civilian employee of the U.S. Army at San Carlos, are sketchy. Although historian Dan Thrapp claims that "the Kid was Al Sieber's creation," this is doubtful. Kid would have learned his scouting and trailing techniques from his grandfather, not from Sieber. In his biography Thrapp relies heavily on secondary accounts but admits that their facts about Kid and Sieber are questionable. Britton Davis, who commanded scouts at Fort Apache, explained the process of selecting scouts by commanding officers. "The sergeants and corporals were appointed by [Captain] Crawford from the chiefs and prominent men."[18] Sieber was a civilian scout with no power either to enlist or assign rank to Apache scouts: that duty was reserved for the officers who commanded them. No doubt Sieber deployed Apache scouts in the field; however, he did not appoint them. H. B. Wharfield, who commanded Apache scouts in the Tenth Cavalry at Fort Apache in 1918, suggests that it is very likely Sieber "did not know the Apache Kid until after he enlisted." Sieber had only been appointed civilian chief of scouts in May 1882, and since Kid enlisted as a scout the following month, this observation probably is correct. After evaluating the relationship between Kid and Sieber, Wharfield contends that Kid may not have been "as friendly with Sieber as some writers would have us believe."[19]

Thrust into combat at Big Dry Wash in July 1882, Kid quickly gained the confidence of both his commanding officer and Sieber as well as the devotion of the scouts that worked under his control. Kid seemed to have a charismatic aura that drew allegiance, and perhaps he had a self-confident masculine image that attracted scouts to serve and obey him. Apparently during his service in the Big Dry Wash campaign Al Sieber realized that Kid showed exemplary leadership qualities. Kid also seemed to be blessed with extraordinary eyesight. Evidently, with his amazingly keen vision he could see things at a great distance that officers and enlisted men could not even distinguish with field glasses.[20] This may be exaggeration, but an Apache who had lived in the desert all of his life and trained as a scout definitely had an advantage over any officer who would have difficulty seeing slight movements at a great distance that would betray the hidden positions of the enemy. That is exactly why Apache scouts were considered indispensable by the U.S. Army.

Various writers have helped to develop a larger-than-life image of Kid that does not meet the test of investigation. For example, Jess Hayes asserts that by age eighteen Kid "had killed more than twenty of his people."[21] This is unlikely, because Kid did not become a scout until 1882, when he was about twenty-two. During the court-martial, Kid admitted to killing only the man who had killed his grandfather. Kid did see a great deal of action during the Geronimo campaigns, and he probably killed enemy combatants, but we will never know for sure how many. Lieutenant Thomas Cruse, who worked with scouts, remembered Kid as tall and handsome. Kid served with Al Sieber at the Big Dry Wash fight in 1882 and accompanied Sieber and Crook into Mexico after the renegade Juh in 1883. Later, Kid returned with Sieber to Mexico during General Crook's Geronimo campaign in 1885. Lieutenant H. B.

Wharfield reported that Kid also accompanied Captain Emmet Crawford into the Sierra Madre of Mexico in 1886. Kid continued to work as a scout from June 1882 until he was charged with mutiny and desertion and dishonorably discharged on January 11, 1888. No doubt Kid spent months at a time in the field as first sergeant of scouts and gained the loyalty and respect of his scouts. Kid also gathered a great deal of information about the geography of the Sierra Madre that would aid him after he became a renegade.[22]

During the 1880s Kid's dilemma was interconnected with the different truths accepted by the army, the Apaches, and the white population in Arizona. Kid represented that very small minority caught in the nebulous zone between conflicting societies that viewed local knowledge and truth from different perspectives. As will be shown, Kid's mistake was his decision to enforce the socially accepted Apache custom of retribution by killing the man who had murdered his grandfather. It was the Apache thing to do, but it happened when he was supposed to be on duty as a scout at San Carlos. Although this killing had met with approval among the Apaches, he had also broken army rules by leaving his post for five days. Once his reprisal had been accomplished, Kid could not escape the web of power that quickly surrounded him. When you factor in hostile attitudes and prejudice against Apaches and two alien legal systems, army and civilian, operated by whites, you have a real dilemma that could not be avoided or, in Kid's case, resolved. No matter what he did it would have been impossible for him to receive a fair trial from either the military or civilian criminal justice systems. Kid was not the only Native American to suffer in this ambivalent existence. Plenty Horses, Nahdiezaz, and other Indians who had been forced to attend Carlisle Indian School found it almost impossible to survive after returning to the reservation.[23] They were considered to be neither Indian nor white, stuck in the middle between two different cultures.

The difficulties faced by Kid in trying to adjust to white society and its restrictions during the late nineteenth century were incessant and formidable. Apaches shared few common values with whites, which greatly disadvantaged their efforts to acclimate to the changes brought on by the Arizona territorial government and the U.S. Army. They also suffered because of prejudice against them and a belief that Apaches were more savage, ruthless, treacherous, and barbaric than other Indians. Territorial governors, newspaper editors, and members of the U.S. Army called for their elimination either by exile or extermination. Under such circumstances Apaches such as Kid never really had a chance. Switching from Apache society to white society and back again confirmed that they always would be Apaches. No matter how competent a scout he was, the white public mistrusted Kid and others like him. Becoming a renegade confirmed the worst about Kid and the rest of the Apaches; they could not be "civilized."

Kid's troubles in the U.S. Army started in late May 1887 when a series of events led him on an odyssey through three different legal jurisdictions—Apache, military, and civilian. Unfortunately, with only a few government documents, military dispatches, and sketchy, unreliable secondary sources to rely upon, the origins of Kid's family feud with SA band member Rip remain a mystery shrouded in a time gone by that has spawned legends and inaccurate stories about Kid. Apparently, Rip killed Kid's grandfather, SI band chief Togodechuz, in December 1886. After the killing Kid refused to become the band chief; consequently, fellow band members selected Gonshayee. As second choice for chief it is possible that Gonshayee felt defensive, and it soon became apparent that he was not a good leader, with some band members refusing to obey him. After brooding over the death of his grandfather for several months, Kid may have been goaded into taking action by Gonshayee. Kid left his duty station without permission and engaged in a three-day drinking party with band members. After consulting with Gonshayee, Kid and a group of well-armed men traveled south to Aravaipa Canyon and killed Rip in an Apache tradition that had been accepted by military officers.[24] This triggered a series of dramatic events that soon began the saga of the legendary renegade, Apache Kid.

After being arrested, convicted, imprisoned, and then released by a military court, Kid was once again arrested and convicted and sentenced to seven years in prison by a territorial court. As already noted, in 1889 Kid escaped from custody while being transported to Yuma and remained at large for the remainder of his life. In the evocative words of historian Dan Thrapp, "Those disappearing tracks, at first so fresh and hot and now so cold and faint, were the last solid clues that the forces of law and order would ever have to the Apache Kid."[25] Thrapp characterized the story of this maverick as a tragedy; however, if Kid had not been absent without leave from San Carlos when he killed a man we would know virtually nothing about him. At best, he might have appeared in a footnote in some history book.

In this study we can learn not only a little more about Kid but also, we might hope, much more about the whole tangle of conflicting cultures, personalities, and legal systems that surrounded him. It is not the outcome, but the whole process that included very differing cultural perceptions and changing transitional laws to which Kid was subjected that is illuminating. The intention here is to reveal the vague and contradictory nature of the Apache-white amalgam that surrounded him and complicated his life at San Carlos. Further, it is an examination of the judicial processes on display in Kid's case to discover what they reveal about the confusing liminal world in which Kid lived and, to a lesser degree, the roles of both his accusers and his defenders in three very differing legal systems. This will help us to understand this fascinating, larger-than-life Apache champion who could not be captured or killed.

SAN CARLOS SCOUTS

The longer we knew the Apache scouts, the better we liked them.
They were wilder and more suspicious than the Pimas and Marico-
pas, but far more reliable, and endowed with a greater amount of
courage and daring. I have never known an officer whose experience entitled his opinion to the slightest consideration, who did not
believe as I do on this subject.

JOHN G. BOURKE, *On the Border with Crook*, 203

. . .

John G. Bourke, who served with General George Crook in the
Arizona Territory in the 1870s and 1880s, knew well the value of
Apache scouts. They were absolutely essential in the hunt for renegades
such as Chato, Nana, Victorio, and Geronimo. Indian scouts had been
employed by the U.S. Army since the Revolutionary War. In 1866, at the
end of the Civil War, Congress passed legislation that allowed U.S.
Army commanders in the field to recruit a maximum of one thousand
Indian scouts to help wage war in the American West against any
Indians labeled "hostiles," a term often used to describe those who had
left their reservations. In his discussion on Indian scouts, Colonel
William Winthrop, the leading military law scholar of the day, observed
that Indians had long been recruited and accepted in military service
during times of war. Winthrop argued that Indians, although not citizens, were considered domestic subjects of the United States.[1]

Upon enlistment Indian scouts were required to observe the same military rules as other enlisted men. All recruits swore an oath to obey orders from the President and their commanders according to the Articles of War.[2] Despite this oath most Indian scouts remained unaware of their obligations as soldiers. Although they were considered to be full-fledged members of the U.S. Army, few scouts knew much about their legal status as enlisted men. They knew little about the Articles of War and were not required to wear uniforms or salute officers. Such distinctions placed them in a special category with ill-defined rules and obligations that were never clarified by military commanders or by the application of the Articles of War.

During the late nineteenth century Apache scouts offered U.S. Army units in the Arizona Territory an important military asset to find Apaches who were raiding white settlers in the Southwest. The scouts' knowledge of the raiding methods and customs gave the cavalry an important edge in their attempts to return rebellious Indians to the reservation. Kid became part of an elite group of Apache scouts. He, like other scouts, functioned in a complicated world between Apache society and military culture. It must have been awkward and bewildering for Kid and his fellow scouts to move back and forth without completely understanding what was required of them in a military unit that demanded discipline and obedience to its officers, many of whom were West Point graduates schooled and trained to enforce army rules.

Commanders in the field enlisted scouts for short durations, usually six months, then discharged and reinstated them as their services were required. This provided flexibility for army officers but exacerbated the transient nature of the scouts. During the early 1880s rebellions by Chiricahua leaders such as Nana, Ulzana, Chihuahua, Chato, and Geronimo assured the demand for scouts to force the rebels and their followers to return to San Carlos. From 1882 through 1887 Kid's virtual existence revolved around his position as a scout. Although Kid's enlistments were typical, his appointment as sergeant of scouts at such a young age was unusual. Kid's total enlistment lasted approximately two years and seven months in service. In between these various short enlistments were intermittent breaks totaling one year and eleven months. As a sergeant of scouts he enhanced his reputation among fellow scouts and Apaches at San Carlos as well as among army officers who respected his ability to track and find renegades. Askisaylala, Bachoandoth, Margey, and Nahconquisay, all SI band members and scouts, served with him and obeyed his commands without question. They also enlisted for short durations, averaging about six months in service and six months off.

It was not difficult to recruit scouts, since they received thirteen dollars a month, the same pay as cavalry troopers, and an additional twelve dollars to maintain their horses.[3] Twenty-five dollars in wages on the reservation was good money for an Apache scout, who could purchase items that otherwise would have been unattainable. While serving at San Carlos scouts lived in brush wickiups near the officers' tents. Before battle they normally stripped off most of their clothes and wore only a breech-cloth, an action that adhered to their Apache tribal traditions. Such freedom that existed with poorly understood military rules and Apache constraints must have been very enticing for Kid and his scouts. Leaving the drudgery of reservation life behind for the adventurous work of pursuing renegades did not lead scouts to become fully assimilated. This lifestyle was just enough to modify their Apache ways but not enough to cause true assimilation into military society. Kid lived in a period that included the decline of Apache society and economic and social turmoil resulting from continuing military incursions against the Apaches.[4]

During the mid-nineteenth century, the White Mountain Apaches, the Northern and Southern Tontos, and the Cibecues—all members of the Western Apaches—were living around Flagstaff and Prescott eastward to Fort Apache. The Mogollon Rim is an escarpment between six and seven thousand feet high cut by deep gorges and winding narrow rivers and streams, with trails running steeply up the canyon sides. This high plateau region abounded with thick forests of ponderosa pine, piñon pine, juniper, spruce, douglas fir, oak, and a variety of fauna, including deer, elk, and bear. The Apaches camped along the river valleys below the escarpment, including those of the Verde and the Salt. While rainfall in most of the desert areas of Arizona averaged about ten inches, the Mogollon Rim received over twenty-five inches each year, which allowed Western Apaches to raise crops. They supplemented their diet with venison and piñon nuts, acorns, and the plentiful berries of the region.

After gold was discovered in northern Arizona in 1863, miners invaded the Tonto Apache country. Troops from Whipple Barracks near Prescott killed Apaches indiscriminately, and white miners also attacked, dislodging them from their land. Eventually the Northern and Southern Tonto Apaches were congregated at Camp Verde south of the Mogollon Rim country. In 1871 the federal government established the White Mountain Reservation to accommodate the thousands of Apaches who were uprooted from other regions and forced to relocate. Although the northern region around Fort Apache had abundant game and was well-watered, the southern section around San Carlos was a barren desert that lacked adequate water and vegetation. This reservation project turned into a disaster, and Apaches frequently attempted to escape its oppressive conditions. In 1875 a large number of Tonto and other Apaches were relocated from Camp Verde to San Carlos. Within two years approximately five thousand Apaches were living at San Carlos, many from rival bands that nurtured enmity towards each other.[5]

The dramatic differences between Fort Apache and San Carlos in part foretell the course of the Apache Indian wars. Better resources and climate explain why Fort Apache became comparatively successful, while in the south the Apaches struggled to survive in the inhospitable surroundings of San Carlos. Firsthand observations by Apaches, travelers, Indian agents, and U.S. Army officers explain why San Carlos proved to be a disaster.

Fort Apache, originally called Camp Apache, provided a pleasant environment for the U.S. cavalry. After arriving Lieutenant Thomas Cruse described the natural beauty of his surroundings. The soldiers' barracks, storehouse, and officers' quarters were constructed from wood with stables for the horses. "Cool trout streams ran at the back door . . . and over all loomed the snow-capped White Mountains."[6] In 1883, Herman Ten Kate visited Fort Apache after spending two weeks at San Carlos. He traveled along a rugged mountain path that led him out of the heat of the Gila River valley into a region of cooler air. He observed a wall of mountains covered by a heavy forest. His party followed a twisting and tortuous ascent until they reached a mountain plateau, where they followed one trail surrounded by forests of oak and fir. Moving northward to Turkey Creek, they journeyed onward to Seven Miles Hill before descending into a narrow valley with dense forest growth. In Kate's words, the last miles of the long trek to Fort Apache led them through a landscape "lovely beyond all description."[7]

Fort Apache, situated on a wide, grassy plateau about five thousand feet high, was a far more pleasing environment than hot, dusty San Carlos. Ten Kate described the magnificent view of mountains covered with splendid forests. Looking to the east, he viewed the mighty peaks of Mount Thomas and Mount Ord, both over ten thousand feet high. He observed that the Coyotero Apaches at Fort Apache were cultivating crops on the fertile banks of the valley streams and also gathering large quantities of piñon nuts in the forests. Fort Apache was blessed with an abundance of game such as bears, deer, turkeys, and grouse. The streams were full of trout and other kinds of fish.[8] Ten Kate stated that, compared to Fort Apache, San Carlos was a barren wasteland. San Carlos lacked good water and other resources that were essential to developing a successful reservation to accommodate thousands of Apaches.

During the 1870s and early 1880s, San Carlos Agency was administered by a rapidly changing succession of Indian agents, among them John Clum, J. C. Tiffany, and P. P. Wilcox. In the 1880s the U.S. Army attempted to take control of the reservation because civilian agents often refused to deal fairly with the Apaches. When Captain Francis Pierce became the agent in 1885, his appointment demonstrated that the U.S.

Army had finally wrested control of San Carlos from civil authorities. Following Pierce's appointment, a succession of military officers accepted and served assignments as Indian agents.

The San Carlos Agency buildings, the main center of the reservation, were situated on an arid plain forty-five feet above the Gila and San Carlos rivers; because of the scarcity of water, the landscape lacked shade trees, and vegetation was sparse. Mountain ranges surrounded the reservation, with the Sierra Ancha and Mazatzal Mountains in the northwest, the Pinals toward the west, and Mount Trumbull dominating the southern horizon. The agency buildings, constructed of adobe with shingled roofs, were located near the Gila River. Indian agents often complained about the poor living conditions. Although they were not farmers, the Indian agents, with white farmers assisting, forced the Apaches to establish small farms along the north bank of the Gila River and the banks of the San Carlos River north toward Peridot.

A variety of firsthand observers left vivid pictures of this ill-fated reservation. They were sharply critical of its location, of the inadequate housing, of the civilian Indian agents who managed it, and of the quantity and quality of the food provided by the government. When Herman Ten Kate arrived at San Carlos in 1883, he saw numerous Indian wickiups and the soldiers' white tents sprawled along the San Carlos and Gila rivers. Interspersed among them were a series of small structures and two large, ugly buildings: the agency and the officers' quarters. A handful of other agency buildings included a slaughterhouse, stores, and the guardhouse used to house prisoners. Ten Kate noted that the adobe buildings were in a state of disrepair and decay. During the two weeks at San Carlos, Ten Kate developed a low opinion of civilian Indian agent P. P. Wilcox. According to Ten Kate, Wilcox "was callous, rude, brutal toward his subordinates, and . . . he hated and despised the Indians."[9] Wilcox, who had become a shareholder in the trader's store operated by his son-in-law, was much hated by the Apaches. Like many Indian agents, he was more concerned with bettering himself than helping the Apaches.

Ten Kate complained about serious and enduring problems between whites and Indians: the failure of the federal government to honor treaties, widespread fraud committed by Indian agents, and the infringement of Arizona's white settlers and miners upon Indian rights. Ten Kate, with the aid of French photographer C. Duhem, photographed Loco, Nana, and other chiefs. Ten Kate observed that many of the Apaches had a great sense of humor and loved to play games and dance.[10] This native sense of humor demonstrates that despite the crowding, exploitation, terrible environment, and dismal conditions at San Carlos, some aspects of Apache culture remained alive and well.

During the 1880s the commissioner of Indian affairs and the Indian agents put a positive spin in their annual progress reports about the work of "civilizing" the Apaches to assure Congress and the President that the government's Indian policies were succeeding. In his 1880 report, Agent J. C. Tiffany told the commissioner that the Apaches wanted to educate their children in the white man's ways and that they had been asking for the establishment of a reservation school. Tiffany claimed that the Apaches were attempting to become farmers: they had constructed irrigation ditches and were growing small fields of grain. The Indian agent, however, complained that the Apaches became easily discouraged when their efforts at irrigation failed.[11] Traditionally hunters-gatherers, the Apaches were poor farmers. Tiffany concluded that agriculture could not be satisfactorily pursued at the San Carlos Agency without the development of a series of dams and irrigation ditches. There was little arable land, he admitted, except along the Gila River. Most of the Apaches cultivated small fields of wheat and corn that ranged from five to thirty acres.[12] In his 1884 report, Agent P. P. Wilcox reported that the Apaches had built fourteen new dams across the San Carlos River and were producing large quantities of grain. These reports, written to please the commissioner of Indian affairs, painted a rosy picture of the progress being made at San Carlos.

Other observers, such as Asa Daklugie, a Chiricahua Apache, were far more harsh in their assessment of existing conditions at the agency:

"San Carlos! That was the worst place in all the great territory stolen from the Apaches. . . . Where there is no grass there is no game."[13] Military officers also painted a more realistic picture of the depressing conditions on the reservation than the glowing reports of the civilian Indian agents. For example, Lieutenant Thomas Cruse, serving with Apache scouts, judged that "San Carlos was such an undesirable place, a barren waste no Indian would have stopped in, voluntarily."[14] Lieutenant Britton Davis, assigned to handle Apache scouts, may have said it best when he observed that "San Carlos won unanimously our designation . . . as 'Hell's Forty Acres.'"[15] During his tenure at the agency Davis observed that everywhere there were the "sullen, stolid, hopeless, suspicious faces of the older Indians challenging you." Idleness created discord among the Apaches, who had lived for centuries unrestrained throughout the Arizona Territory. According to Davis the Apaches' principal occupation was to gather "once a week at the Agency to receive their rations."[16] Davis's observations about life at San Carlos underscore the ravages of culture shock. Older Apaches resented and resisted forced relocation and the pernicious efforts to eradicate their ways of life.

Captain Francis Pierce, who assumed control of San Carlos Agency in 1885, had been born and raised in New York and had served as a captain with the New York Volunteers during the Civil War. On March 13, 1865, he received an appointment to brevet brigadier-general of volunteers. He had led his troops in several successful Civil War military engagements and had himself been wounded in a fight against General James Longstreet. After the war, Pierce received a regular commission in 1866 as second lieutenant in the First Infantry. In 1880 he was promoted to captain. When Captain Pierce assumed control of San Carlos as Indian agent in September 1885, he had over nine years of experience with the Lakota, Walapai, and Apache Indians.[17]

In 1885 the Congressional Committee on Expenditures for Indians visited the Indian reservations in the American West to determine what steps should be taken to "civilize" and bring the Indian into American society. Many congressmen were under intense pressure to open up reservation land to settlement by farmers and ranchers. A major goal of the committee assigned to visit reservations was to formulate recommendations that would include allotting land in severalty to Indian families and building schools for Indian children to help break the old tribal traditions. Chaired by Congressman William S. Holman, the committee visited San Carlos Reservation in October 1885. Holman asked Captain Pierce a variety of questions to determine conditions that existed on the reservation. Pierce, an honest observer, reported that the Apaches had difficulty raising crops. Heavy rains during monsoonal periods often carried away dams; some dams had to be rebuilt six times during one very rainy summer. Because of such hardships, the Apaches were able to cultivate only about eleven hundred acres. Aware that conditions at San Carlos were ill-suited to farming, Pierce advised the congressional committee that no more than six thousand acres should be irrigated. Irrigation canals were dug by the Apaches, who often became discouraged with their meager harvests. When asked by Holman whether dividing land among the Apaches would be feasible, Pierce explained that there was not enough arable land to provide "40 acres to each head of a family." Most Apaches had a cow or two; however, there was not enough grassland at San Carlos to feed them. Consequently, they were usually fed hay grown outside of San Carlos. Pierce strongly urged Congress to provide a mill that would allow the Apaches to grind their own grain for flour, because it would save the government money.[18]

The congressional committee learned that there were no school buildings on the reservation; however, some forty boys and five girls had been sent to Carlisle Indian School in Pennsylvania. These educational statistics are remarkable considering the large number of Apaches living at San Carlos. Why were there so few students available for school? Equally vexing, why did the congressional committee members fail to ask Pierce about the low number of children attending school? In a discussion about the living quarters for the Apaches, the committee learned that only one Indian had a regular home: the rest lived in wickiups.[19] Three years later, Captain John L. Bullis, the new Indian agent, discovered that only eight families lived in houses. One reason for this was cultural; when an Apache died in a wickiup, a band member immediately burned it down in the belief that the dead person's spirit would haunt the dwelling. In obedience to tribal customs, Apaches refused to build substantial houses.[20]

Observers offered some interesting details about how thousands of Apaches at the agency received their weekly government rations. Every Thursday the cattle used to supply the Indians were slaughtered. On Friday the Apaches lined up to receive their weekly rations of beef, which were given to the head of the household or the band leader. In 1886 these rations amounted to about one-third of their provisions; the remainder the Apaches produced on their own.[21] On ration day large groups of Apaches arrived at San Carlos from distant camps to collect their allotted meat and sacks of flour. They purchased other items from the agency store. C. T. Connell, employed to complete a census, colorfully described the scene at San Carlos: "Ration day is a gala one for the many tribes, who are denoted by their dress, cut of the hair, paint upon the face, style of clothing and actions, and there is a mingling of Tontos, Coyoteros, Pinals, and Apache-Yumans." Each person received approximately five and one-half pounds of flour, four ounces of beans, eight pounds of sugar, four pounds of coffee, and one pound of salt.[22] These rations, with the exception of beef and beans, contained very little nutritional value. Agents contracted to provide supplies for the Apaches had some ingenious ways to increase their profits. Cattle sellers usually let their herds drink large quantities of water before weighing them. Those providing other essential food items often purchased insect-infested items at reduced prices. Agents also short-weighted their food items to increase profits. Consuming substandard food with minimal nutritional value increased the Apaches' suffering.

In 1886, despite the absence of real acculturation among the Apaches,

Captain Pierce expressed satisfaction with the progress being made at San Carlos.[23] Two years later, however, the new agent reported that many Apache men refused to work and were restless and rebellious. Signs of assimilation were few. A few Apaches were beginning to wear "civilized garments," while others dressed "in full modern apparel." Several years later, agriculture had allegedly increased, with the Apaches cultivating one thousand acres of land.[24] The deprivation of reservation life made the restless young male Apaches susceptible to being recruited to serve as U.S. Army scouts. Such work seemed to be the only government-sanctioned avenue to escape the confines of San Carlos.

In 1871, when General George Crook first arrived in Arizona, he quickly learned that Apache military strategy was difficult to combat, and hiring Apache scouts became the best means to locate and defeat renegades. Captain John Bourke, Crook's aide, explained why Apaches were such skilled opponents. When pursued by the cavalry, Apaches scattered like "quail, and then hovered on the flanks of the whites, and were far more formidable when dispersed than when they were moving in compact bodies."[25] Apaches adopted the best military policy: they wore out the enemy by vexatious tactics that typically resulted in a fruitless chase. Apaches knew where to find food; they also knew the location of water holes and springs. The cavalry could not match their resourcefulness, and some soldiers might "wander about, half-crazed with thirst, and maddened by the heat." Captain Bourke, who became an authority on Western Apache culture, understood that Apaches were in no sense cowards but "never lost a shot, and never lost a warrior in a fight where a brisk run across the nearest ridge would save his life and exhaust the heavily clad soldier who endeavored to catch him."[26]

Bourke explained that Crook gained insights about Apache military tactics: "An Indian in his mode of warfare is more than the equal of the white man, and it would be practically impossible with white soldiers to subdue the Chiricahuas in their own haunts." The Chiricahuas and

other Apache tribes knew every foot of their territory; they could endure
fatigue and fasting for extended periods that few white soldiers could
match. Crook discovered that in combat the Apaches remained hidden
from sight while the soldiers, pursuing the enemy, had to expose themselves.[27]

The challenge of U.S. military officers was to locate the "hostiles"
without being seen. This could be accomplished only by using Apache
scouts, who knew the enemy's habits and methods. Apache scouts were
able to advance at night, always keeping a sufficient distance ahead of
the main body of troops to provide protection against an ambush. This
enabled them to discover the enemy position without being exposed to
fire. Apache renegades could detect any unusual movement of a bush;
the fall of a rock or the glint of the sun from weapons would send "hostiles" flying in all directions, eluding their pursuers. Crook concluded
that under such conditions the best strategy was to return to San Carlos,
wait until things had quieted down, and then repeat the military opera-
tion.[28] He realized that the only hope of success in fighting them was to
use their own methods and their own people against them.

Although Crook admired and respected the fighting skills of the
Apaches, he had ambivalent feelings about them culturally. For example,
in his report on the problems with the Chiricahuas, Crook stated that
they were instinctively wild, fierce, savage, and brutal and would not
hesitate a second before taking an opponent's life. He referred to them as
"tigers of the human race." According to Crook, Apache scouts' ani-
mallike virtues included "vision keen as a hawk's" and a gait "stealthy as
the panther's." Crook judged the Apaches to be the "fiercest and most
formidable of all our Indians, when on the war-path," yet he also
expressed admiration for them. He observed in a letter, "I do not hesitate
to put the Apache at the very head for natural intelligence and discern-
ment."[29]

In Arizona, General Crook employed Archie McIntosh, an experienced scout, part Scot and part Chippewa, in 1871 to help recruit Apache
scouts. After holding talks with Coyotero Apaches at San Carlos, Crook

recruited a number of scouts and organized a company under the command of Captain Guy V. Henry. Crook understood the importance of using Apache scouts in campaigns against various Apache tribes. By offering them employment, horses, weapons, and other inducements, he convinced them that it would be to their advantage to cooperate in waging war against other White Mountain Apaches and Chiricahuas who had been their enemies for decades. Crook conducted successful raids against recalcitrant Apache bands throughout central Arizona, subduing them and forcing them to relocate to San Carlos. Despite efforts to control the Apaches in the central and northeastern part of Arizona, the White Mountain Apaches and Tontos continued to cause trouble, and Crook finally began an offensive against them in the winter of 1872 that ended in their defeat. As soon as he conquered one group, he immediately recruited some of the band members to serve as scouts in other military campaigns. It was an effective strategy that paid dividends. Captain Bourke recalled that the Apache scouts were relentless and proved to be ruthless with any renegade Apaches who resisted them. After one scout had been killed in a fire fight, "another expedition went out to the scene of the fight . . . came up on the Indian camp, and killed the whole party, regardless of age or sex."[30] Apache scouts could be unforgiving.

During his offensive of 1872 Crook issued an order "requiring all Indians to report immediately to their agencies or be regarded as hostile." In December 1872 Crook held a meeting with various Apache leaders at San Carlos, and SL band chief Eskiminzin promised to provide aid in hunting down the "hostiles." Soon afterward, Crook recruited thirty-one new scouts, including many Aravaipa Apaches. Some of the best known scouts included Alchesay, Machol, Blanquet, Chiquito, Kelsay, Kasoha, Nantaje, and Nannasaddi. Crook ordered Captain William H. Brown to employ these scouts to hunt down Delshay and Chunz, two of the most notorious Apache leaders.[31] Nantaje, who knew the country well, explained to the captain that he was pretty sure where the renegades would be holed up and led Brown's column slowly up the "slippery, rocky, dangerous trail" alongside the canyon until they discovered the hostile Apaches camped in a formidable position among the bluffs of the Salt River. Brown's party of scouts found a small pony herd and above them spied a huge cave that offered cover to the renegades. Brown's troops themselves used large boulders for cover and fired into the mouth of the cave. Several groups who tried to escape the cave were cut down by withering gunfire. Another company of men were able to reach a cliff above the cave and rolled huge rocks down upon the "hostiles." During this fierce fight, a small boy wandered into the line of fire. Nantaje jumped forward, grabbed the boy by the arm, and jerked him to safety. Bourke remembered that "Our men spontaneously ceased firing for one minute to cheer." When the troops overran the enemy position, they found fifty-seven bodies piled in the cave and took twenty women and children prisoner.[32]

Bourke, who served as Crook's aide during the early campaigns against the Apaches, kept a diary detailing troop movements and the use of scouts. In December 1872 he received a dispatch that Archie McIntosh's advance guard had found Apache renegades and exchanged fire. Two weeks later, ninety-eight Pima Indian scouts helped a unit surprise the enemy, killing at least twenty-five near Tonto Creek. By that time most of the military units led by officers had upwards of forty-six scouts each serving with them.[33]

During the winter of 1872–73, General Crook launched numerous expeditions against renegades. With the aid of the scouts, Crook's army traveled over twelve hundred miles, killed five hundred hostile Indians, and forced the rest to surrender and march to San Carlos. Because of their loyal service and devotion under fire, Crook recommended ten of them for the Congressional Medal of Honor. Although initially disapproved, they were eventually confirmed on April 12, 1875. Sergeants Alchesay and Jim and privates Nantaje, Machol, Blanquet, Chiquito, Kelsay, Kasoha, Nannasaddi, and Elsatsoosn were the recipients. Four were listed as Sierra Blanca Apaches, and six claimed to be Aravaipa Apaches.[34] The bravery exhibited by these scouts probably was best exemplified by Nantaje's quick actions while saving the child at the cave battle. All the scouts had risked their lives under dangerous circumstances, and Crook believed that they deserved to be honored for their service to the army. The Medal of Honor, established in 1862, was a distinguished award bestowed only on a select few. The following year commissioned officers became eligible to receive the award. During the Indian campaigns, 1861–98, a total of 419 Medals of Honor were awarded to enlisted men and officers.[35] Nearly half of those were awarded for gallantry during actions against the Apaches. It is quite remarkable that ten Apache scouts received this award during one campaign and that others would also receive the award.[36] Captain Bourke, Lieutenant Cruse, and General Nelson Miles also received this award.

In testimony before the Congressional Committee on Expenditures for Indians, Crook detailed the harsh methods he used to subdue renegade Apaches during his winter campaign. Crook stated that he began to attack the White Mountain Apaches in December 1872 and concluded his offensive on April 6, 1873.[37] During that period he organized as many as eight expeditions against them in the Tonto Basin and Mogollon Rim country. Unfortunately, returning them to San Carlos did not resolve all of his problems with them. On May 27, 1873, Lieutenant Jacob Almy was killed at San Carlos while trying to break up a disturbance among these same Apaches. An infuriated Crook especially "wanted the heads" of Delshay, Chunz, Cochinay, and Candesi, who had been implicated in the killing and remained at large. Crook was determined that none of the "hostiles" who returned to San Carlos would be allowed to surrender without bringing in the offending chiefs. Several of them returned and begged to be allowed to remain at San Carlos. Crook testified to the committee: "After I got them scared good, I told them, there is but one condition on which you can stay on this reservation, and that is to bring in heads of certain Indians."[38] To assure his success, Crook placed a bounty on the heads of the dissident Apaches. The heads of Chunz and six others were delivered to San Carlos on July 25 by a group of Apaches led by Desalin. Indian Agent John Clum remembered that just after breakfast five Apaches walked into his office carrying a gunny sack. They untied the sack and rolled seven heads out on the ground.[39] Desalin returned a few days later with the head of Delshay, one of the instigators in the outbreak.

Considering that Crook subscribed to the philosophy of the Friends of the Indians, a group that supported rights for Native Americans, his ruthless policies towards the Apache renegades seem out of character. The Friends of the Indians, a pro-Indian lobby group led by Herbert Welsh, Henry Pratt, George Bird Grinnell, Henry Dawes, and other reformers, advanced both land allotment in severalty and education of Indian children to break down their tribal traditions.[40] In retrospect, Crook's ruthless methods against the Apaches brought quick results, but at a terrible price. Critics claimed that it was little better than the Mexican government's methods of paying bounties for Apache scalps. Nevertheless, many white residents of Arizona probably viewed Crook's policies as a way of ridding the land of troublesome Apaches.

Despite their usefulness in hunting down renegades, the hiring of Indian scouts remained controversial during the late nineteenth century. Apache scouts were not universally accepted by U.S. cavalry officers. However, Crook, Bourke, Emmet Crawford, Charles Gatewood, and Britton Davis, officers who spent a great deal of time in the field with their scouts, had only good things to say about them. Other officers serving in the field during the Apache wars were more ambivalent and never fully trusted or accepted Apache scouts. Medical officer Leonard Wood had an opportunity to observe the skills of scouts on many occasions and claimed, "Our Indians did some wonderful tracking . . . keeping the trail for miles, when it seemed to be all washed out."[41] On another military adventure, however, Wood complained that some scouts had gotten drunk and wanted to go off and kill some Mexicans. Wood was unaware of the reason that many Apaches hated Mexicans: the Mexican government had offered bounties on Apache scalps for decades. Many officers in the field showed no interest in learning Apache customs and history.

Although the Apache scouts were effective, some command officers debated their value and never accepted the scouts as necessary. Generals Nelson A. Miles and Phil Sheridan "distrusted the scouts' motivations and loyalty," especially after the mutiny of White Mountain Apache scouts at Cibecue in 1881, a rebellion to be discussed in chapter 2. This mutiny convinced many officers that the scouts would not be loyal in a crisis. Crook understood that Cibecue was an anomaly; indeed, there were no other scout mutinies during his service in Arizona. He continued to recruit them despite criticism and protests within the military and was convinced that "the scouts were responsible for every successful encounter with the Apache enemy."[42]

Crook became so absorbed in his Apache scouts that he preferred their company to that of his own officers. Lieutenant Colonel Richard Irving Dodge, one of his officers, complained that Crook treated Ranald Mackenzie, a fellow officer, and himself shabbily but would spend hours "chatting pleasantly with an Indian or a dirty scout." Bourke also displayed a deep interest in Apache culture, writing later that while on a campaign nearly all of the talk he had was with the Apache scouts. Officers like Bourke, Britton Davis, Crawford, Gatewood, and Crook virtually lived with the Apache scouts when they were on the move. Bourke had praise especially for Alchise, Chiquito, and Nantaje.[43]

Fighting "hostiles" continued sporadically in the late 1870s until July 1882, when a group of Apache renegades refused to submit to control, fled the reservation, and ambushed and killed Cibecue Charley Colvig, San Carlos chief of police. This band of Apaches selected Natiotish as their leader and fled north into the Mogollon Rim area near Big Dry Wash, where they prepared for a showdown with the army. Lieutenant Thomas Cruse, assigned to the Sixth Cavalry, was accompanied by Al Sieber and his Apache scouts. Cruse recalled that Kid and his scouts led Sieber down narrow Diablo Canyon into the Chevelon's Forks area, a region with steep cliffs and a narrow trail climbing out of the Tonto Basin. Sieber concluded that Natiotish and his band would stop here. Natiotish believed that, being high above the advancing army, he and his

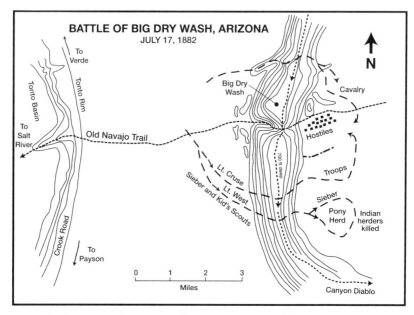

Battle of Big Dry Wash, Arizona, July 17, 1882. Courtesy Melodie Tune, graphic artist, Instructional Technology Services, San Diego State University

Apaches would have a superior position. About 3:00 p.m. Sieber and the scouts slowly crept up the canyon rim from the south and discovered the Apaches waiting in ambush about seven hundred yards distant on the opposite side of the canyon.[44] Sieber, with First Sergeant Kid and his Company A scouts, circled far to the right and came up on the Apaches from the rear. When Natiotish's Apaches spotted Sieber and his scouts, they opened fire. With some clever maneuvering Sieber's scouts reached the pony herd of the enemy and caught the guards looking in the other direction. Kid and his scouts quickly killed all of them, rounded up the pony herd, and drove it to the rear to prevent Natiotish's men from escaping. By this time other troops had arrived and began firing into Natiotish's stronghold. In the thick of the battle Cruse remembered that Sieber had killed at least six or eight "hostiles." Mistakenly assuming that Sieber had killed all of the renegades, Cruse headed into the camp.

Sieber shouted for him to wait, but Cruse and some of his men rushed in and came under heavy fire. Although several soldiers were killed, Cruse survived and later received the Congressional Medal of Honor for his heroism. Cruse reported that out of a total of seventy-five warriors, no more than fifteen survived. Natiotish was among the dead. The army suffered some casualties, including Private Pete, one of Kid's scouts in Company A. Later, Pete's name was listed with the other fallen cavalry troopers on the battle monument erected to commemorate the lives lost during the fighting.[45] The Big Dry Wash fight proved to be the last major conventional battle with the Apaches in Arizona Territory. However, other skirmishes with the Chiricahuas would follow. Crook's army would have to pursue Geronimo into Mexico several times before the wars with the Chiricahua Apaches would finally end.

On September 4, 1882, after serving several years in the Great Plains wars against the Lakotas and Cheyennes, General Crook received orders to return to the Arizona Territory and command the Department of Arizona. Geronimo had fled San Carlos for Mexico, and General Phil Sheridan believed that because of Crook's extensive experience with Apaches he was best qualified to deal with these renegades. Upon his return Crook discovered that Geronimo and other Apaches were conducting raids from their bases within the Sierra Madre of Mexico all over southeast Arizona and western New Mexico. They continued to be a problem for Crook throughout the period 1882–86; consequently, he began vigorously recruiting Apache scouts. Hunting down Geronimo would require a large number of scouts. Crook placed Captain Emmet Crawford in control of 193 Apache scouts, while Lieutenant Charles B. Gatewood, Captain Wirt Davis, and Lieutenant Britton Davis commanded approximately 100 scouts each.[46]

While fighting against Apache renegades, Kid and his scouts adhered to tribal customs. Apache warriors eschewed military uniforms and instead normally wore a breechcloth or trousers, long-legged buckskin

moccasins, and sometimes a bright calico shirt. To distinguish themselves from the "hostile" Apaches they wore red bands around their
heads. The scouts carried only the barest essentials, normally a rifle, car-
tridge belt, canteen, and knife. To protect the cavalry, Apache scouts
were placed several miles in advance of the main party to prevent surprise attacks.

Just before launching a major campaign against Geronimo, Crook
sent Crawford and his scouts to scour the Mogollon Rim country to
make sure that there were no Chiricahuas hiding in that region.
Crawford found none, reported to Fort Bowie, and prepared to enter
Mexico. In May 1883 Crook and four groups of scouts, including Kid,
entered the Chiricahuas' Sierra Madre stronghold. Crook had gained the
confidence of Peaches, a Chiricahua scout who knew Geronimo's
haunts, and led the command right into one of the abandoned camps.
The "hostiles" had a tendency to decamp regularly to prevent surprise,
but Crook's command quickly made contact with them and launched a
surprise attack on Chato's camp. This assault shocked Geronimo and
other band chiefs, who had believed their stronghold to be impregnable
against intrusions by Mexican or American troops. Within a few days
Geronimo and other Chiricahuas surrendered to Cook. This successful
campaign ended when the bands led by Geronimo, Chato, Nachez, and
Chihuahua returned to the San Carlos reservation. Upon his return,
Chato agreed to scout for Crook and was assigned to Lieutenant Davis's
Company B, stationed at Fort Apache. Chato's decision reveals once
again the value of hiring Apache scouts who knew where the enemy
could be found.

In 1885, when Geronimo and his band once again escaped San Carlos
and fled to Mexico, Crook employed over five hundred scouts to pursue
them across the border into the Sierra Madre. As before, these scouts
were deployed into four groups commanded by Crawford, Davis,
Gatewood, and Wirt Davis. Kid, who had reenlisted in June 1885,
directed a group of scouts in Crawford's command that pursued
Geronimo into Mexico. During these two incursions into Mexico, Kid

gained valuable information about the Sierra Madre that would prove useful in his later years. During this campaign Captain Crawford was killed in December 1885 by Mexicans who attacked his group, allegedly thinking they were Apaches. The angry Apache scouts opened up on the Mexican troops, killing the officer who had shot Crawford along with several other soldiers. After some tense minutes the two sides finally ceased fire, and the Mexican troops withdrew. Despite the loss of Crawford, Crook's tactics of using Apache scouts paid off when Geronimo and other chiefs agreed to talk with him at Cañon de los Embudos just across the border in Mexico. After they agreed to surrender, Crook and the main body of Apaches headed north back to San Carlos. Geronimo had agreed to return to the reservation, but after crossing into the Arizona Territory he and a few followers lingered just north of the border and began drinking liquor, probably mescal, provided by a whiskey trader. On March 28, 1886, Geronimo, who knew about Crook's strict policy against drinking, fled south to Mexico with about thirty-five band members.[47]

General Sheridan was outraged by this turn of events, and an embarrassed Crook, seeing his position as untenable, sent a letter of resignation and asked to be reassigned to other duties. He was replaced by General Nelson Miles, who continued the war against Geronimo's band. Both Miles and Sheridan "had no confidence in the Indian scouts." Both generals had become exasperated with the idea that regular troops could not hunt down and destroy renegade Apaches without the help of scouts.[48] Viewing the Apache scouts as untrustworthy, Miles immediately discharged most of them, keeping only a few to follow the trail of the "hostiles." He ordered Captain H. W. Lawton to lead a contingent of regular cavalry troops in pursuit of Geronimo. After a period of six months, during which Lawton's troops never made contact with Geronimo or other Apache renegades, Miles finally realized that Lawton and his men could not effectively trail and find Geronimo without the aid of Chiricahua Apache scouts. Miles ordered Lieutenant Charles B. Gatewood to pick two scouts to accompany Lawton's troops and find

Geronimo. Gatewood selected Kayitah and Martine, both Chiricahua Apache scouts, to assist him on this dangerous expedition. They entered the Sierra Madre and located the Chiricahua camp. Geronimo, realizing that his options were limited, agreed to parlay. Gatewood remembered that Geronimo was the last renegade to arrive at his camp; he laid his rifle down, came forward, and offered his hand in a gesture of conciliation.[49] The Chiricahua leaders sat in a semicircle and began to talk. Gatewood advised Geronimo to surrender and said he would be sent with his band members to Florida. If Geronimo refused to surrender, Gatewood explained, his band would have to "fight it out to the bitter end." The meeting broke up and reassembled later after Geronimo consulted with members of his band. The Chiricahua chief, who trusted Gatewood, ultimately agreed to meet with General Miles just across the border in Arizona Territory, where he finally surrendered.

On September 8, 1886, General Miles placed Geronimo and all the Chiricahuas, including the scouts, on a train bound for Florida. Chato, Kayitah, Martine, and other loyal Chiricahua scouts who had served faithfully with Crook and Gatewood felt betrayed as they were sent into exile. Miles showed no concern for them and claimed all of the glory for being the man who had "captured" Geronimo. Gatewood, who had put his life in great danger, became Miles's aide but received no recognition for his service against Geronimo and failed to gain promotion throughout the rest of his military career.[50]

We have seen that Kid, while a young man in his early twenties, was part of an extraordinary era of Apache versus Apache, skillful Indian men bargaining with a very recent enemy to hunt down and kill other Apaches, such as the Chiricahuas, whom they viewed as ancient foes. The actions and tribulations of Kid can help us understand the conflicts he and other scouts felt in this time of unclear cultural boundaries and values. Kid exhibited the same confusion that plagued other scouts, none of whom ever completely understood their responsibilities to the U.S. Army. Instead, these scouts carried most of their Apache traditions into this foreign cultural milieu and were forced to conform with rigid military rules, including the Articles of War, which included 128 complex military rules. How could Kid or any of his scouts possibly comprehend them? Ultimately, the conflicts between his inability to understand these rules, his loyalty to his own Apache heritage and its expectations, and his responsibilities to his military superiors would lead him down a path of self-destruction. A series of remarkable events would end with charges against him for desertion and mutiny, both punishable by death if found guilty by courts-martial. These dramatic episodes would eventually catapult him into the limelight.

— 2 —

KID'S AMBIGUOUS WORLD

PURSUING THE HOSTILES

Lieut. Johnson's command surprised a murderous band of Apaches in the Rincon Mountains at noon Saturday capturing their baggage and horses. The Indians scattered among the rocks, and evidently will try to make their way back to San Carlos. . . . The troops are still in sharp pursuit.

New York Times, June 14, 1887

.   .   .

Kid, a first sergeant, directed his scouts not only during campaigns but also when they were acting as policemen at San Carlos. This was the scouts' main duty after Geronimo's surrender in 1886. Both Kid and his scouts were required to obey their military commanders and a myriad of army rules while serving their enlistments. Equally important, Kid was bound by Apache tribal custom, which was confusing to outsiders, including army officers. If someone killed a member of his SI band, Kid or some other band member had to avenge the murder. This could be done through negotiation or retribution; if these means failed, the band members would lose face within the community. The Western Apaches perceived homicide as a problem to be resolved by the clan or band. Chiefs were respected for their ability to conduct successful raids and for their leadership, but if they failed to satisfy the majority, they could be deposed. This diffuse leadership style may explain why the Western Apaches developed social control mechanisms that paralleled the

Comanche concept of homicide as strictly a family matter. With the Apaches, however, the clan acted as the family. If someone raped an Apache's wife, her husband would immediately attempt to kill the other man, and public sentiment would support his actions.[1]

Blood feuds, common within Western Apache culture, created a certain amount of instability. Like other social groups, Apaches sometimes held grudges and believed in "getting even." Once the loss became "equal" the feud could end, but sometimes it escalated. To some extent Apache social controls for homicide paralleled the feuding tradition prevalent within Mediterranean societies of Sicily, Sardinia, Corsica, Italy, and Montenegro. Among the Apaches the wronged party might ambush the perpetrator without warning. Homicides were often avenged during or following drinking parties, where, under the influence of alcohol, old grudges might be recalled and settled. On numerous occasions Indian agents at San Carlos complained of the violent nature of these drunken sessions. For example, in 1889 Indian agent Captain John L. Bullis declared that drinking bouts plagued the reservation and often ended in the killing of one or more participants. While completing research in the 1920s, Grenville Goodwin discovered that interband killings often happened when men were gambling or quarreling over women, and most of the killings occurred during or following drinking parties.[2] In his study of the Western Apaches Goodwin explained that if one man had killed another, the assailant would carry weapons for protection, thus hoping to prevent an ambush.

The clan nature of feuds was paramount: the opposing party became the enemy of the entire extended clan, not just the immediate family. Feuds were resolved in multiple ways. If the killer was known as a troublemaker, his family might refuse to defend him and give him up. The killer might flee the area and remain away until the bitterness against him and his crime subsided. When killings occurred, the family of the aggressor had the duty to resolve the dispute between the two families. The leader of the clan would try to arrange for compensation to right the wrong committed by his band member. Not surprisingly, hostility between feuding clans often smoldered for years and sometimes flared up again, resulting in a rival killing as payback. This helps to explain killings that occurred years later during or after drinking parties.

After an accidental killing the aggrieved party often made attempts to get even. To prevent this, the killer had to pay compensation demanded by a brother or other close relative. Such payments would usually be in the form of horses, blankets, buckskin, or similarly valuable items. Refusal often exacerbated a feud. The mother of the guilty party often played an important role in the negotiations. Chiefs and other prominent clan members might also become involved in the discussions between the two families. The family of the killer had to offer an agreed-upon payment to the aggrieved party: "The payment was either burned on the spot or taken home and used. If the horses which were given as part of the payment were killed, their meat was eaten."[3] Although their belief systems were quite different from those of the dominant white society, the Apaches possessed deep-rooted moral values and a sophisticated code of behavior designed to control social and criminal behavior. However, the Apache moral code was unacceptable to the Arizona territorial officials, who made little, if any, effort to understand the nature of Apache beliefs and who refused to tolerate retaliation killings as a form of social control. Although based on centuries of tradition, Apache customs were deemed incompatible with white society.

Until the 1880s the federal government allowed Indian tribal members to dispense their own form of justice within reservations. With the Crow Dog murder trial in 1881, however, that practice began to change. As the federal government pushed Native Americans off their land and into reservations in the American West, problems arose as to which legal system, tribal or federal, had the authority to prosecute Indians accused of committing crimes on reservations. The issue of whether local tribal governments had the power to resolve murders became paramount in the fall of 1881 at the Rosebud Agency in the Dakota Territory. An ongoing feud had been simmering between two prominent Brulé Sioux leaders on the reservation. On August 5, 1881, as Spotted Tail rode along a road, Crow Dog, standing by a wagon, allegedly "sprang up with his rifle and shot him in the side." The wound proved fatal. A Brulé council meeting resolved the killing by applying the tribal tradition of negotiations between the two parties. Crow Dog agreed to give the Spotted Tail family "a payment of $600, eight horses, and one blanket." In the opinion of legal historian Sidney Harring, "Brulé law effectively and quickly redressed the killing and restored tribal harmony."[4]

White citizens of Dakota Territory, however, were outraged by this turn of events and called for the arrest and prosecution of Crow Dog for murder. In late March 1882 the Rosebud Agency Indian agent ordered Hollow Horn Bear to arrest Crow Dog and place him in the custody of U.S. authorities at Fort Niobrara. Prosecuted within the U.S. District Court of Dakota Territory in Deadwood City, the Crow Dog case became an important trial because a central question was at stake: Who had authority to control crime on the Rosebud Agency, the Brulé tribal council or the federal district court? Like other Native Americans prosecuted in the American West, Crow Dog faced an all-white male jury that the U.S. prosecutor quickly impaneled. The entire trial required only a day and a half. Defense council A. J. Plowman called Crow Dog to testify on his own behalf. The defendant claimed that he had stopped to repair his wagon and a few minutes later Spotted Tail galloped up and aimed a revolver at him, at which point Crow Dog fired his weapon. After closing arguments and instructions from the judge, the jury, in spite of the complexity of the case, hastily returned a guilty verdict. A day later, Judge G. C. Moody sentenced Crow Dog to death by hanging.[5]

In 1883, in *Ex Parte Crow Dog*, U.S. Supreme Court Justice Samuel F. Miller issued a major unanimous decision in favor of the Brulé Sioux tribal council: they did indeed have the power to resolve major crimes committed at the Rosebud Agency. After careful analysis of the treaties made with the Indians and the federal regulations governing reservations,

the U.S. Supreme Court ruled that the U.S. District Court had no jurisdiction over crimes committed upon a reservation. The court issued the
writ of *habeas corpus* requested by petitioners' lawyers, and two years after
the original guilty verdict, the defendant was released. Historian Sidney
Harring notes that during the nineteenth century when the U.S.
Supreme Court heard criminal appeals, many decisions were reversed
because of the appalling quality of criminal justice administered in the
frontier areas. The Supreme Court believed that "death penalty convictions had to show a level of integrity difficult for frontier justice." Crow
Dog's release outraged many U.S. citizens, who protested to Congress.[6]

Until the Crow Dog case, the federal government had accepted
Indian tribal control and punishment of criminal offenses that occurred
on reservations. Sections 2145 and 2146, Title 38, of the 1874 revised U.S.
statutes stated that although all federal laws "shall extend to the Indian
country," they do not apply to Indians committing offenses in Indian
country who have been punished by tribal law.[7] This acceptance of tribal
punishment, however, was about to change. Under intense pressure by
territorial officials and settlers in the American West, Congress enacted
the Major Crimes Act. Section 9 of the Indian Appropriation Act of
March 3, 1885, placed a series of major crimes under the control of the
federal and territorial governments. The law stated that "all Indians,
committing against the person or property of another Indian or other
person . . . murder, manslaughter, rape, assault with intent to kill, arson,
burglary, and larceny within any Territory of the United States, and
either within or without an Indian reservation, shall be subject" to the
laws of the territory and will be tried the same as all other persons
charged with such crimes within the exclusive jurisdiction of the United
States.[8]

With the passage of the Major Crimes Act, Congress dramatically
reduced tribal sovereignty and increased federal and territorial control of
Indian reservations. Crimes committed by Indians on reservations or
regions nearby were now decided by federal and territorial criminal justice systems. The first challenge to the Major Crimes Act came the fol-

lowing year with *U.S. v. Kagama* (1886). The U.S. Supreme Court allowed that "the nature of the offense (murder) is one which in most all cases of its commission is punishable by the laws of the states, and within the jurisdiction of their courts." However, the court concluded that the "Indian tribes *are* the wards of the nation. They are communities *dependent* on the United States." The legal discussions focused narrowly on the powers of the federal government to regulate the affairs of Indians on reservations; the individual constitutional rights of the Indian defendant were not considered. The ruling of the U.S. Supreme Court only upheld that Congress had a right to pass the Major Crimes Act of 1885 to control behavior on Indian reservations; therefore, it was a valid law.[9] The court did not rule, however, on whether U.S. district or territorial courts had jurisdiction over criminal cases. This court decision clarified criminal jurisdiction by placing seven major crimes (including homicide) that occurred on Indian reservations under the control of federal courts.

It should be noted here that Crow Dog's case fell under the jurisdiction of civil authorities, whereas Kid's problems would be resolved initially under military law. The killing of one Apache by another appeared to be of little concern to military officers at San Carlos. On the other hand, civilian authorities perceived blood feud killings as murder. In 1887 U.S. District Court authorities prosecuted Captain Jack and four Apache band members for killing rival Apaches in retaliation for an earlier murder.[10] The Captain Jack cases indicated that guidelines concerning legal jurisdiction over Native Americans and the prosecution of Apaches and other Indians were unclear.

There was a strong connection between the Major Crimes Act of 1885 and the Dawes Act of 1887. Both Congressman William S. Holman and Senator Henry L. Dawes authored the Indian Appropriations Bill, which included a clause to place all Indians who committed one of seven major crimes on reservations or within territories under jurisdiction of the same courts used to try U.S. residents. Equally important, both officials supported a bill to open up "surplus"

Indian land to white settlers. These two laws also coincided with the movement for an Indian Commission to oversee the planned dismantling of reservations. As noted in chapter 1, Congressman Holman chaired the Committee on Expenditures for Indians that visited and collected information on the various reservations, including San Carlos, for drafting the new law. Holman's committee was the precursor to the yet to be established Indian Commission that would manage the affairs of reservation Indians. The commission would enforce new federal policies that included reducing the size of reservations, allotting land in severalty, decreasing expenditures and annuities, establishing schools for Native American children to "civilize" them and eradicate their cultural traditions, and finally, creating and enforcing new laws to punish Indians.[11]

During this era (1885–89) federal and local governmental relationships with the Indians were rapidly changing. This helps to explain why Kid's legal status for crimes committed on or off the San Carlos Agency was murky: in the 1880s various Indian rights were steadily being eroded. There is no doubt that an imperfect transformation was in progress. Federal, state, and territorial laws were in a state of flux, and many legal issues on the status of Indian defendants would not be resolved until 1889.

Kid's rude introduction to military law began soon after a tiswin party among fellow members of his SI band of Apaches. Tiswin, an alcoholic beverage made from corn, was popular among the Apaches during the nineteenth century. In the 1880s Indian agents at San Carlos Agency experienced significant difficulty trying to aid Apaches in adjusting to federal control. By 1886 numerous Apache bands had been confined to the reservation, where they were unable to follow their lifestyle of raiding for cattle and horses. One can only imagine the difficulty they must have experienced in giving up the horse for farming in narrow strips of unproductive land along the San Carlos and Gila rivers. To escape the effects of culture shock, San Carlos Apaches turned more and more to alcohol as a way to relieve the oppressive drudgery of subsistence farming.

Exactly when the Apaches first used tiswin is unclear; Morris Opler believes that the beverage may have been inspired by indigenous people from the northern provinces of Mexico.[12] Apaches also consumed mescal and other beverages, but tiswin remained their favorite drink. The brewing process normally required several days to prepare a beverage with an alcohol content of 4 percent. Women proficient in making this drink were in demand. The women usually would put ground corn into a pot and boil it for several hours until the water was reduced by half. Next they would refill the container with water and boil it again until the mixture was a few inches from the top. Then the liquid was strained off, cooled, and placed in large water jars. Normally the jars were covered to allow rapid fermentation. To give the drink a little "kick," women sometimes added jimsonweed root (*Datura stramonium*), often called loco weed, to their boiling brew. Apparently the women had determined the proper amount of jimsonweed to use, because large quantities of this plant can be lethal. Apaches discovered that in small quantities jimsonweed, because of its ability to bring about a relaxed state and to induce hallucinations, provided an added dimension to tiswin.[13] In the twentieth century Apache women began to use yeast to increase the fermentation process. Captain John G. Bourke, an acute observer of Apache behavior, discovered that tiswin "figured prominently in all the Apache ceremonial dances and preparations for the warpath." He learned that the Apaches were so fond of tiswin that they ignored or defied all ordinances made for its suppression. After studying the rituals of medicine men, Bourke concluded that tiswin was "their sacred intoxicant."[14]

In his 1886 report Captain Francis Pierce, Indian agent at San Carlos, complained that before drinking, "the bucks fast two or three days while the tiswin is making." Under such conditions the drink will produce the "most frantic intoxication."[15] Drinking episodes sometimes turned into wild melees resulting in fights and frequently ending in death. U.S. authorities refused to accept Apache customs, and tiswin drinking created problems for virtually all Indian agents and military officers trying to keep the peace. Indian agents at San Carlos complained that the Apache men refused to be broken of the tiswin habit. For example, Indian Agent J. C. Tiffany reported in 1880 that Indians had been wounded in fights caused by tiswin parties. During that year one man was killed near Fort Apache, and Chief Juh was stabbed with a knife.[16] The San Carlos reports, however, provide only sketchy, incomplete statistics on the actual numbers injured and killed. Although one fatality was reported in 1880, the following year five men were reported killed, and several tiswin parties ended with violence and serious injuries. In 1886 Captain Pierce complained that five violent deaths had occurred that year because of tiswin parties. From 1887 to 1889, Indian agents admitted that there were numerous reports of tiswin parties resulting in violence and injury; however, the numbers killed were not reported. In 1889 Captain John L. Bullis also reported that tiswin drinking was resulting in fights and killings. While examining the use of tiswin, Frederick Lloyd, acting assistant surgeon at San Carlos, discovered that fasting for four days before drinking created rapid intoxication. In Lloyd's opinion, tiswin was the most frequent catalyst for disputes among Apaches.[17]

After first hearing about the tiswin problems, General Crook ordered Lieutenant Britton Davis to put a stop to tiswin drinking. Reflecting the dominant values of the times, the general concluded that tiswin parties "resulted in two things, a 'bad Injun,' and a hang-over for the next two or three days." Davis recalled that after he tired of making ineffectual threats against tiswin, he arrested an inebriated Apache and placed him in the guardhouse. During a discussion about tiswin Davis was confronted by an inebriated, belligerent Chihuahua. When Davis informed the Apache that General Crook had forbiden the use of tiswin, Chihuahua replied, "We all drank tiswin last night, all of us in the tent and outside, except the scouts; and many more. What are you going to do about it? Are you going to put us all in jail? You have no jail big enough."[18] Chihuahua's comments that the scouts did not drink suggests that he understood the scouts' special situation. Under army rules they could be severely disciplined for drinking tiswin. Finally, an exasperated Davis sent a telegram to Captain Pierce at San Carlos complaining about the tiswin drinking problem and requesting instructions on how to proceed. Upon receiving the plea, Pierce woke up Al Sieber, chief of scouts, and asked him for his opinion. Sieber replied: "It's nothing but a tiswin drunk. Don't pay any attention to it." Sieber, who had been drinking himself that night, went back to sleep.[19]

During the early 1880s Lieutenant Davis spent a great deal of time with the Chiricahua Apaches and eventually understood how some of them felt about criticism of tiswin drinking. At Fort Apache, Davis convinced several chiefs to talk to him about the tiswin problem. He began by criticizing the Apache custom of wife beating: "Old Nana got up, said an angry sentence or two . . . and stalked out of the tent." Davis insisted that his Apache scout Mickey Free translate exactly what Nana had said. Reluctantly Free replied, "Tell the *Nantan Enchau* (stout chief) . . . that he can't advise me how to treat my women. He is only a boy. I killed men before he was born."[20] Nana, then in his eighties, had only three years earlier fled San Carlos with only a handful of men and women and led a famous raid that frightened settlers and exhausted the U.S. Cavalry in a series of brief engagements. Davis understood Nana's words and observed that when the Apaches had made peace with the Americans

> nothing had been said about their conduct among themselves; they were not children to be taught how to live with their women and what they should eat or drink. All their lives they had eaten and drunk what seemed good to them. The white men drank wine and whiskey, even the officers and soldiers at the posts. The treatment of their wives was their own business. . . . Now they were being punished for things they had a right to do so long as they did no harm to others.[21]

Nana knew that Apache rights were under assault by military and civil authorities and was trying to protect tiswin drinking, a sacred ancient tradition. Tiswin, however, caused many Apache breakouts and created turmoil at San Carlos, forcing the U.S. Cavalry to pursue the renegades with Apache scouts. In 1887, when Kid participated in a drinking party, he not only violated military rules but also crossed a cultural line by acting as an Apache instead of a scout. By doing this, Kid, an acknowledged leader of his young Apache scouts, failed them.

The Apache Indian wars from 1870 to 1886 saw only one scout mutiny against military authority before Kid's alleged mutiny. During the nineteenth century white civilians and military personnel had always considered Apache medicine men to be bizarre and unsettling; consequently, officials sometimes panicked when they learned of spiritual ceremonies to cure the sick or to make potent medicine. Captain Bourke remembered that during General George Crook's 1872 campaign, a young Apache known as Nochaydelklinne served as a scout. The soldiers at Fort Apache called him Bobby Doklinny.[22] About a decade later, Nochaydelklinne had become a medicine man. Called the "dreamer" by his followers, he had established himself as a powerful religious leader at Cibecue. In 1881, when he began a ceremony in an attempt to revive two chiefs killed in a tiswin drunk, he created a great deal of consternation among the soldiers and reservation administrators. The San Carlos Agency officials and the army panicked because they did not understand the practices of Apache medicine men. After some discussion with military authorities, Agent Tiffany requested that the medicine man come to San Carlos to practice his medicine. Nochaydelklinne refused, claiming that the presence of white men had inhibited the power of his medicine.[23] The medicine man also asked the white soldiers to leave Cibecue. This exasperated the Indian agent, who requested General Eugene A. Carr to go to Cibecue to arrest the medicine man.

Observing the influence of the medicine man upon his Apache

scouts, Lieutenant Thomas Cruse complained to his commander that the scouts were becoming harder to control and that he heard threats made by White Mountain Apaches that if the whites did not leave Apache country they could be driven out. Lieutenant Cruse informed General Carr that his scouts wanted to be loyal; however, if a showdown occurred they might side with the medicine man. Cruse recommended using other scouts composed of Mojaves, Yumas, and Chiricahuas, who had no loyalty to the medicine man, to calm down the situation.[24] For reasons unknown, Carr ignored Cruse's sensible suggestion.

At 4:00 p.m. on August 28, 1881, General Carr assembled his officers and asked them to read his orders from the department commander. Carr was ordered to "capture or *kill* Nochaydelklinne!" The general expressed concern that such action would exacerbate the situation and might cause a revolt by the medicine man's followers. When General Carr's column of troops formed a line in front of the medicine man's camp, Sánchez, a belligerent and hot-headed leader, and several other Apaches rode up to meet them. The general ordered Nochaydelklinne to return with him to San Carlos; the medicine man refused. Carr ordered Mose, a scout, and Sergeant McDonald to take Nochaydelklinne into custody and protect him. Cruse remembered that during Carr's discussion with the medicine man, a large number of Indians began to assemble around the meeting place. Cruse observed that others were also gathering on the mesas all around, and many had stripped down for fighting. Suddenly, Sánchez and several others raised their rifles and fired: "Instantly, at least a hundred other shots roared." Dandy Jim, one of Cruse's Apache scouts, shot and instantly killed Captain Hentig; Sergeant McDonald immediately shot Nochaydelklinne. The continuing fire forced General Carr and his troops to retreat; his losses included at least eight troopers.[25] It was a disaster that could have been avoided.

Article 58 of the Articles of War, dealing with jurisdiction of crimes during war, explained that an act committed during Indian warfare "may be said to have been committed in a 'time of war'" and was punishable by a court-martial. Whether a "state of war" existed or not would not affect the applicability of a court-martial. On the other hand, military tribunals would be suspended if the state of war had ended.[26] Although only Congress has the right to declare war, presidents sometimes bent the rules and provided their own definition of a state of war. In August 1881 military authorities in the Arizona Territory applied Article 58 to prosecute Apache scouts accused of mutiny at Cibecue Creek. Dandy Jim, Dead Shot, and Skippy, three of Lieutenant Cruse's scouts, were arrested and ordered to stand trial. In three separate court-martial cases, defense counsel Second Lieutenant E. F. Willcox failed to challenge a single member of the nine-person courts. Whether this failure was because of his inexperience in military law is unknown, but this inept legal strategy certainly reduced his clients' chances. Willcox did, however, question whether the charge of murder against Dead Shot was legal. He noted that under Article 58 such a charge could be made only "in time of war and at other times only by civil courts of criminal jurisdiction."[27]

In his legal opinion to Secretary of War Robert T. Lincoln, Judge Advocate General David Swaim expressed concern about this argument. He wondered whether Dead Shot, the defendant, had been correctly charged and questioned whether the evidence was "sufficient to show that a state of war existed" as specified by the Articles of War. He noted that "hostilities [did] not appear to exist" during the mutiny at Cibecue and concluded that if this was the case "the charges of murder," for which the prisoner had been convicted, "should not be approved." Swaim also questioned whether the scout Dead Shot was "a duly enlisted soldier" in the U.S. Army. He reported to Lincoln that the Articles of War had not been "read or explained to" Dead Shot and the other two scouts. Finally, Swaim argued that if no proof existed that the three men had been "duly enlisted," then the "court-martial had no jurisdiction and the prisoners" should be tried "for murder in the criminal courts of the Territory."[28] Despite a strong argument by Swaim, Secretary Lincoln was not persuaded, and the death sentences were confirmed by President Chester A. Arthur. On March 3, 1882, the three scouts were hanged at Fort Grant, and two other scouts were sentenced to Alcatraz.[29]

These were the only cases of mutiny by Apache scouts during the Indian wars. In General Crook's opinion, had other scouts been used who were not from the medicine man's camp, Nochaydelklinne would have been arrested and the killings would not have occurred. It was unfortunate that white authorities failed to understand Apache religious traditions or find a way to defuse a dangerous situation. Albert Reagan, an anthropologist who studied and observed medicine man rituals practiced among the White Mountain Apaches at Fort Apache in the 1920s, claimed that Nochaydelklinne had practiced the wheel dance, a frenzied ceremony, at Cibecue in 1881. After observing one of these wild, exuberant performances, Reagan claimed that he could understand why whites might have become alarmed.[30]

General Carr's inability to grasp that the spiritual rituals of Nochaydelklinne were relatively harmless led to the mutiny at Cibecue. The inept military attempts to capture the Apache medicine man turned into a fiasco that created unrest among the White Mountain Apaches for several years. The Cibecue mutiny had set a legal precedent that is relevant for understanding what happened to Kid. The mutiny made U.S. Army officers stationed in Arizona Territory very uneasy and reopened the debate on whether they should be using Apache scouts in their commands.

As noted earlier, Kid was required to respect two sets of codes, the military regulations designated in the Articles of War and the cultural customs of his own Apache band. On the one hand he had to obey the orders of his commander; on the other, tribal customs required that he take revenge against the man who killed his grandfather. According to a popular legend, as a very young man Togodechuz, Kid's grandfather, won the affections of a girl over Rip, a rival from the SA band.[31] Consequently, Rip sulked and continued to plot for years to get even. This festering resentment between Rip and Kid's grandfather suddenly erupted at a drinking party in Aravaipa Canyon on December 25, 1886, when Rip encouraged his brother, Gonzizzie, to kill Togodechuz. SI band members immediately retaliated by killing Gonzizzie, but that did not satisfy Kid, who knew that Rip had been the one responsible. Over the years Rip had earned a bad reputation in Aravaipa Canyon; he had either killed or goaded fellow band members into killing at least two, possibly more, Apaches from rival bands. Rip gloated about his murders, boasted about never being charged with a crime by either Apache or civilian legal authorities, and threatened to kill Kid. Killing a band chief such as Togodechuz, of course, made the crime extremely infamous and alarming for other Apaches living in Aravaipa Canyon, because it put SA band members at risk for retaliation. This killing resulted in a blood feud between the two bands that, by Apache custom, had to be answered with retaliation.

H. B. Wharfield, a former army officer with experience handling scouts in Arizona, explained that Kid held a grievance against Rip because he had killed Togodechuz, Kid's grandfather, during a drunken brawl six months earlier. One obscure newspaper item in the *Arizona Silver Belt* did in fact report that an Apache had been "killed below the Agency last Monday night, during a tiswin drink."[32] Since Aravaipa Canyon is about twenty-five miles south of San Carlos, Togodechuz may have been the victim of this Christmas Day killing in 1886. General Nelson Miles relates a similar story in his report about Kid's being charged with desertion and mutiny. Whatever the circumstances, sometime after the death of Kid's grandfather, Rip apparently threatened to kill Kid as well. Tom Horn, a scout working at San Carlos, remembered that Sieber cautioned Kid not to retaliate against Rip.[33] Torn between military and tribal duties, Kid chose to break the former and follow the latter.

On May 28, 1887, with Captain Pierce and Al Sieber away for a few days at Fort Apache, Kid and four of his scouts ignored their duties at the San Carlos guardhouse and left the reservation without permission to join band members in a tiswin party that lasted two or three days. It is possible that Gonshayee, the SI band chief and a somewhat sinister figure, influenced Kid to do this. There is little doubt that Kid felt he should avenge his grandfather's death; nevertheless, leaving his duty station at that particular time was ill-advised. On May 31 Kid and his group rode south to Aravaipa Canyon. Upon reaching the camp of Chiquito's SA band, Kid found Rip and shot him to death.[34] In effect Kid had administered the retributive law followed by most Apaches and formerly accepted by the federal government. Despite his belief that under Apache tradition he was right to kill Rip, Kid and his fellow scouts still felt it necessary to submit themselves to army authority. No doubt Kid must have been somewhat apprehensive when he turned himself in, but apparently he believed that Captain Pierce, his military commander, would be fair in administering punishment for leaving his post.

At about 5:00 p.m., on June 1, 1887, Gonshayee, acting as a negotiator, arrived at San Carlos and explained to Captain Pierce that Kid wanted to talk to him. Pierce recalled, "I told him that he could come if he pleased and that the sooner he came the better it would be for him."[35] Gonshayee delivered the message, and within a few minutes Kid and his four scouts, Askisaylala, Bachoandoth, Nahconquisay, and Margey, rode up to Al Sieber's tent, dismounted, and prepared to surrender and accept their punishment. They were accompanied by Gonshayee and about a dozen SI band members mounted on horses, some armed with rifles. They watched attentively as Captain Pierce ordered Kid and his scouts to turn in their rifles and gun belts. All five scouts complied by placing their weapons on the ground and their ammunition belts on a table in front of the tent. Then Captain Pierce ordered them to go to the "calaboose," meaning the guardhouse.[36] Kid testified at his court-martial that Antonio Díaz, the interpreter, spoke to them in Apache, warning, "All the Indians that don't obey the orders will be sent to Florida." At this crucial moment Díaz pointed south "making a circle in his hand which stood for island." This alarmed the SI band members. As Kid explained later, during his court-martial, "I thought those outside thought then that we Scouts would be sent down to Florida."[37] Pierce remembered, "I saw a few men on horseback who were bringing down their fire arms and getting cartridges from their belts. I shouted 'look out Sieber they are going to fire.'"[38] This was followed by more shooting, and a member of Gonshayee's band, probably Miguel, fired a shot that hit Sieber in the ankle. The five scouts fled on foot, while Gonshayee's SI band members continued to fire before riding out of the agency south toward the Gila River. Díaz, of course, was just another employee with no real authority, responsible only for accurately translating the conversation between Kid and Captain Pierce. Apparently, Díaz disliked Kid and may have threatened him with exile in Florida. It is doubtful, however, that he realized what might happen when he made this declaration. His actions led to the wounding of Sieber, the alleged mutiny, and a raid by SI band members into southern Arizona. The surrender must have been an anxious moment for the apprehensive Apache scouts, who had expected to receive justice, and for the SI band members, who were concerned about what would happen to their comrades. With the removal of Geronimo and other Chiricahua Apaches, including the Chiricahua scouts, to Florida the previous year, Diaz's statement had great shock value.

After the shooting, Kid and his scouts switched from their military to their Apache mode of thinking. Accompanied by Gonshayee and about fifteen others, Kid fled San Carlos and headed south. Since they needed more horses, the band members headed out on a raid to secure mounts so they could better elude the military units following them. Apache raiding had a long historical tradition that probably began with the introduction of the horse into the Southwest. The Pueblos, Pimas, and Papagos were the first victims of these early raids by Apaches that focused on taking corn and other commodities. Later, when the Spanish invaded the Southwest, the Apaches stole horses, cattle, or other possessions in numerous raids. Normally a raiding party included ten or twelve band members. Members of the raiding party could enhance their stature within the band by participating in sorties against the enemy. In his examination of the Chiricahua Apaches, Morris Opler observed that

Apache raiding was "the special interests of those who have supernatural power to find or frustrate the enemy."[39]

Apache band chiefs held only nominal power and sometimes could not control the behavior of their clan members. Chiefs were chosen for their ability to lead raiding parties, and they were respected only if they provided strong spiritual power and skilled military leadership. If Gonshayee did not satisfy the majority or if his tactics proved ineffective and resulted in casualties, it was conceivable that another warrior could come forward and lead the band. On Thursday, June 2, seventeen Apache renegades, some on foot, were reported to be near Mount Turnbull and heading south. By the next day Kid and Gonshayee had split their raiding party into two groups.[40] The first raiding party of about ten men, led by Gonshayee, moved southeast along the San Pedro River looking for horses. They arrived at a ranch near Mammoth Mill in the Bunker Hill Mining District the next day. At about 3:00 p.m., Askisaylala, Nahconquisay, and Gonshayee slipped in behind William Diehl, who was chopping a tree. Gonshayee pulled a pistol and shot Diehl to death. Later, in testimony at Gonshayee's murder trial, Vacasheviejo testified that he heard gunfire. Asked if he knew who had killed Diehl, he replied that Gonshayee claimed that he had killed the man with a revolver.[41] Why the SI band chief killed Diehl is unknown; it is possible that Gonshayee did it to impress other band members. After firing several shots at a second man, who took refuge in a cabin, the Apache raiding party hastened to a nearby ranch, roped nine to twelve horses from a corral, and fled. Then they headed southwest, crossing the San Pedro River seeking refuge in the Santa Catalina Mountains just north of Tucson.[42]

The second raiding party, probably led by Kid, with Sayes, Miguel, Margey, and others, split off from Gonshayee's group, crossed Aravaipa Creek, and moved southeast into the Galiuro Mountains, where they stopped to rest. Two days later, on Sunday, June 5, the U.S. Army pursuit group from Fort Thomas, led by Lieutenant Carter P. Johnson of the Tenth Cavalry, spotted a plume of smoke from a campfire in the Santa

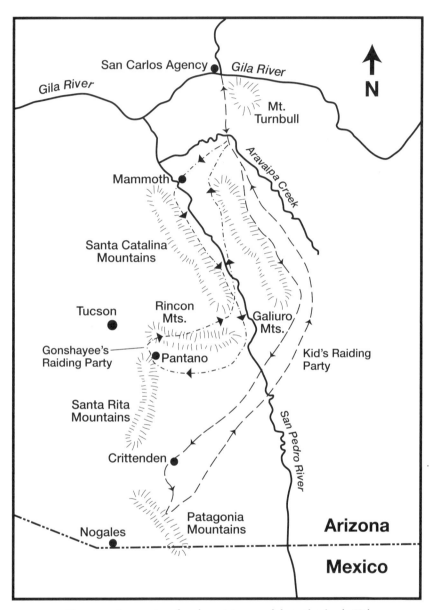

The mountainous region of southern Arizona and the trails taken by Kid and Gonshayee on their raid in 1887. Courtesy Melodie Tune, graphic artist, Instructional Technology Services, San Diego State University

Catalina Mountains that was soon answered by a similar signal fire in the Galiuro Mountains about twenty-five miles to the east. The use of smoke signals to communicate with other bands on a raid had become a common practice among Native Americans in the American West. Morris Opler discovered that smoke signals were often used to determine whether an approaching group were friends or foes. When a party of men sees another in the distance they light a fire and send up a column of smoke, as if to ask, Who are you? The other group will build a fire to answer the first.[43] By June 5, Lieutenant Johnson and four Apache scouts were following the trail of Gonshayee's raiding party toward the Santa Catalina Mountains. An experienced officer who had worked his way up from private to lieutenant, Johnson had honed his skills hunting Apaches by helping to track down and capture Mangas in 1886.

Further east from Gonshayee, Kid's raiding party left the Galiuro Mountains, proceeded down Sulphur Springs Valley, and turned southwest, traveling over one hundred miles to Crittenden, a small settlement less than twenty miles north of the Mexican border. A U.S. Army dispatch reported that on Wednesday, June 8, "one or two Indians who had left the main party" had killed Michael Grace in Temporal Gulch, an isolated area in the Santa Rita Mountains about six miles southwest of Crittenden. After an unsuccessful gun battle with William Leek, who lived near Grace's property, Kid's band of raiders fled southeast and were sighted heading for the Patagonia Mountains less than twelve miles away. Captains H. W. Lawton, Hatfield, and Martin each led troops in pursuit of the second raiding party.[44] These two killings by the raiders created fear among settlers in southeastern Arizona Territory. The Tucson *Arizona Weekly Citizen* reported that the Apaches had gone on the war path: "By the killing of Diehl on the San Pedro and Grace in the Santa Ritas they proclaim their bloody mission and must be hunted to death."[45]

On Friday, June 10, Gonshayee's party, which had been traveling south from the Santa Catalina Mountains, turned north two miles west of Pantano. They moved toward the Rincon Mountains to seek refuge and take a much needed rest. In Gonshayee's group seven were on horseback and four others were still on foot. About noon the next day Lieutenant Johnson and his scouts, pushing hard in pursuit, surprised the renegades' camp on top of the Rincon Mountains. Gonshayee and his band scattered down the mountains on foot carrying only their weapons. The next morning all signs indicated that they were moving north and heading back to San Carlos. Another U.S. Army dispatch from General Nelson A. Miles claimed that en route Gonshayee's raiding party "passed several herds and unprotected ranches without committing any depredations." General Miles was informed that the pursuing party, led by Johnson, determined that the raiding party was badly rattled and anxious to return to San Carlos.[46]

On June 13 General Miles left headquarters and proceeded to San Carlos "to personally inquire into the circumstances attending the disturbance and to direct the movements of the pursuing forces."[47] Either Kid or Gonshayee sent a dispatch by courier to Miles saying that Kid "wanted to come in, but couldn't do it with Johnson crowding him so hard."[48] This dramatic turn of events may have influenced the general to be lenient with Kid. Acting upon this information, on Thursday, June 16, General Miles sent a dispatch to his field officers that "there will be no necessity for any more troops to move further north at present." Meanwhile, pursuing the "hostiles" northward, Johnson's scouts struck trail again where they had crossed Aravaipa Canyon.[49] Johnson reported that Gonshayee's party were heading back to San Carlos. By this time General Miles had arrived at San Carlos to deal personally with an Apache raid that was creating fear in the Arizona Territory. On Saturday morning, June 18, Ashkoelgo left Gonshayee's party and was the first to reach San Carlos and surrender. Miles ordered him put in the guardhouse. Ashkoelgo was released two days later when he agreed to provide information on the raiders. He stated that Gonshayee and his raiders were shaken and wanted to give themselves up to military authorities. Ashkoelgo explained that Gonshayee wanted the troops to stop chasing his raiding party; "your pressing them so close has scattered them."[50]

Gonshayee and four San Carlos SI band Apaches in Florence, Arizona, 1888.
Courtesy Arizona Historical Society, Tucson, AHS #30415

Ashkoelgo argued that if the troops pulled back the Apaches would come in on their own accord. In the meantime, Kid's raiding party had been "reported near Elgin," about twenty miles east of Crittenden, over one hundred miles south of San Carlos.

On Wednesday, June 22, Gonshayee rode into San Carlos and surrendered with seven members of his band. Acting as mediator, Gonshayee talked to General Miles and reaffirmed that Kid wanted to surrender as well. Miles informed Gonshayee that Kid should turn himself in immediately, a message that was delivered in person to Kid by Gonshayee. Three days later on Saturday, June 25, the second raiding group arrived at San Carlos. Kid, Gonshayee, Vacasheviejo, Sayes, Miguel, Margey, and two other band members gave up their weapons and surrendered to Captain Pierce. By voluntarily returning, Kid had agreed to submit to military law and accept his punishment. Kid believed that he had not done much harm and that he would be treated fairly by General Miles. The aftermath of Kid's court-martial suggests that the general felt that since Kid had honored their agreement and returned of his own volition he deserved a fair hearing with appropriate punishment. The next day, June 26, General Miles sent a final dispatch to his officers in the field reporting that Lieutenant Johnson had driven the renegades back to the reservation, where they had surrendered.[51]

*

Being aware of military and governmental policies and the general acceptance of Indian retributive law, General Miles and Captain Pierce did not view Kid's killing of Rip to be of great importance; they were mainly concerned with maintaining military discipline. Miles understood the difficulties faced by the scouts employed at San Carlos. Although Kid had violated the Major Crimes Act of 1885 by killing Rip, Miles felt that killing was justified. Miles understood Kid's dilemma of trying to shift back and forth between two contradictory legal systems. In a dispatch to his commander in San Francisco, General Miles reported: "Although the scouts do not fully comprehend the responsibilities of their obligations as enlisted men, I ordered a general court-martial for their trial, the same as if they had been white soldiers."[52] Miles understood that Apache scouts moved between the opposing worlds of the military and the Apache. His treatment of the scouts during the legal proceedings indicates that he sympathized with their predicament and his actions were just. In another report to his superiors Miles stated that he believed the "affair was unpremeditated." He concluded that Kid and his scouts had agreed to submit to Captain Pierce and "abide by whatever actions" and punishment he decided upon. They had demonstrated good faith by giving up their weapons.[53] Nevertheless, he demanded that military discipline and punishment be administered in the flagrant case of these scouts, who had defied authority and had left their posts without permission. Consequently, General Miles ordered an investigation and a general court-martial. In his final report on this incident, Miles noted that while on their raid

Gonshayee and other SI band Apaches had killed Diehl and Grace, "which will probably be made the subject of judicial investigation by the criminal courts of the Territory."[54] Miles believed that Kid and his scouts should only answer to courts-martial on charges of mutiny and desertion; they should not be tried in a territorial criminal court for shooting Sieber.

It needs to be reiterated that Kid was submitting to military, not civil authorities. The fate of the other SI band members who had killed two white men during the raid, however, would be settled by federal or territorial authorities in their respective jurisdictions. Although Kid's actions seem minor on a scale measured by the exploits of Ulzana, Nana, or Geronimo, the charges of mutiny and desertion filed against Kid and his four scouts, the death of two settlers, and the forthcoming criminal charges against Gonshayee and three SI band members would have devastating results. Kid would learn that justice for an Apache scout could be very harsh.

MILITARY LAW

In 1919, the Acting Judge Advocate General stated: I contend—and
have gratifying evidence of support not only from the public generally but from the profession—that the existing system of Military
Justice is un-American . . . that it is archaic . . . and that it is a system arising out of and regulated by the mere power of Military
Command rather than Law.

SAMUEL T. ANSELL, "Military Justice,"
Cornell Law Quarterly 5 (November 1919)

. . .

The origins of the Articles of War can be traced back to Roman law,
which allowed generals to control armies with an iron fist. Roman
armies were well-disciplined; any violations of the principal military
rules, such as refusing to obey an order, attacking a superior officer,
desertion, mutiny, or cowardice, called for severe penalties. During a
military campaign these types of violations could lead to disaster. Early
military trials established to punish soldiers for criminal behaviors were
of a very summary nature and less involved than civilian courts. Roman
generals held supreme authority over their legions, and any punishment
administered was usually immediate and drastic. There was no appeal
from a Roman army commander's decision in the field.[1] Some of the
harsh penalties that could be administered under the U.S. Articles of
War of 1874 bear a remarkable similarity to those found in Ruffus's *Leges
Militares*.[2] For example, if a Roman soldier refused to obey his commander, he could be severely chastised, but if he resisted his superior

officer he would be executed. Soldiers who incited mutiny also could suffer the penalty of death.[3] Roman law became the basis for many military codes that were developed during the Middle Ages and into the eighteenth century.

Medieval military law, like Roman law, included the need of kings or generals in the field to have unlimited powers of discipline over their armies. For example, King Richard II in 1385 devised a military code of twenty-six articles to control his armies. Probably the most famous code was designed by King Gustavus Adolphus of Sweden, whose Articles of War of 1621 became the precursor of the British military code. His comprehensive code consisted of 167 articles. The most interesting for our discussion was the last, which required that the Articles of War be read to all soldiers.[4] Gustavus Adolphus's articles were translated into English in 1639, and the new British military code adopted a similar pattern of military law that became firmly established with the passage of the Mutiny Act of 1689.[5] From that period on the British developed and improved their Articles of War, which in turn became the basis for U.S. military law.

One can see a straight line of connection between British military law and the U.S. military code that began to take shape during the Revolutionary War. General George Washington encouraged Congress to adopt the 1762 version of the British Articles of War to maintain control over his newly formed army. These 110 articles, modified to fit the Continental Army's needs, were deemed essential during times of war in order to maintain discipline and to provide the power to punish violators in the army and navy. Congress made only minor changes in the original Articles of War until they were modified in 1874. This new version remained in force until replaced with the *Uniform Code of Military Justice* (UCMJ) in 1950.

The U.S. Constitution gave Congress authority to declare war, to raise and support armies, and to create any laws necessary to carry out the functions of the military. The Constitution also accorded the President, as commander-in-chief, the power to commission officers in the army and navy and to enforce military discipline. In 1879 Congress passed the Army Discipline and Regulation Act, which established rules and procedures for holding courts-martial, and in 1882 the War Office published the first *Manual of Military Law*, which has been used to standardize and assure proper procedures for courts-martial.[6]

During the nineteenth century Colonel William Winthrop became the most noted authority on military law. Born in New Haven, Connecticut, in 1831, Winthrop received his B.A. from Yale University and an LL.B. from Yale Law School. After further study at Harvard Law School he was admitted to the bar in Boston. When the Civil War began, he joined the New York militia, rose quickly in rank, and in 1863 received an assignment to the Bureau of Military Justice in Washington, D.C., where he fulfilled the duties of a deputy judge advocate general for nineteen years. During that period he thoroughly explored the origins of British and U.S. military law and began to develop a manuscript on the subject. His legal opus, *Military Law and Precedents*, published in 1886, became the model for military law through the late nineteenth century and well into the twentieth. Winthrop's marvelously written treatise draws numerous examples of legal precedents from both military and civil law to explain the procedures necessary to administer justice for all soldiers in the U.S. Army. Because of his legal expertise, Winthrop received an assignment in 1886 to teach military law at the U.S. Military Academy, where he remained for five years before returning to the Judge Advocate General's Department. Using classroom conditions, he developed a concise version of his legal writings, *Abridgement of Military Law* (1887), that became the manual used to teach military law at West Point.[7]

In the early 1870s Colonel Winthrop was assigned to rewrite the Articles of War. He brought with him a liberal philosophy on military law. Although his revisions increased the original 101 amendments to 128, Winthrop made only minor changes.[8] The U.S. Army had discovered during the Civil War that the military code proved to be inadequate and added new articles from time to time. In 1874 Winthrop revised the code mainly to add new articles to accommodate the changes involving large armies and their control and discipline. Two new articles, however, provided modest protections of soldiers' rights. Article 70 required that any soldier arrested be brought before a court-martial within eight days. This was an attempt to provide a speedy trial to conform more closely with rights accorded citizens under the protection of the U.S. Constitution.[9] Article 93 allowed either defense counsel or the judge advocate to ask for a continuance in the court-martial proceedings. Despite the addition of these two articles, the military code still did not address the need for further protection of a defendant's rights to correspond with the U.S. Constitution. These occasional revisions that occurred throughout the period 1806–1900 indicate that military law was in transition; consequently, Kid was judged by a legal system unsure of itself.

Military law was not the only venue of legal change during the late nineteenth century; criminal and civil law also passed through a period of revision and adjustment. For example, criminal law included major changes, such as the indeterminate sentence, probation, parole, plea bargaining, and substantive rewriting of criminal codes. An explosion of criminal code changes increased the number of crimes from only a handful to more than three hundred in some states, such as Indiana, by 1881.[10] In civil law the rise of industrial giants brought about a variety of conflicting new laws by state and federal governments to either regulate or provide for *laissez-faire* policies to aid big business. This period created confusion and caused a dramatic increase in the number of criminal and civil cases to be reviewed by state, appellate, and supreme courts. For example, the Supreme Court docket increased from 250 cases per term in 1866 to 1,124 by the end of the century.[11] In 1881 U.S. Supreme Court Justice Oliver Wendell Holmes, Jr., suggested: "The life of the law has not been logic: it has been experience."[12] This certainly would apply to Arizona Territory, where the county courts were just being formed. They had virtually no experience in law, and some cases tried in county courts displayed these weaknesses during the 1880s and 1890s. Justice proved to be harsh for people of color, such as Apache, Asian, and Hispanic defendants. Inadequate protection of ethnic minorities' rights seemed to run parallel in both military and criminal law, as Kid's cases will reveal.

While serving as a judge advocate general, Winthrop advocated changes that would provide every soldier, regardless of rank, with full protection of the law by using concepts similar to those developed within federal and state legal systems, including the right to an attorney. Winthrop also supported a statute of limitations for soldiers charged with desertion. Most commanding officers were inclined to arrest and prosecute soldiers who had deserted but who had not been apprehended until many years later. It should not be surprising that Winthrop's ideas were not universally accepted by many U.S. Army officers.

The conservative school of military law that stood in opposition to Winthrop's liberalizing efforts was led by General William T. Sherman, who believed in the discipline-first, justice-will-follow school of military law, and he was not alone. Although he had legal training, Sherman did not trust the influence of civil law in the military realm. In 1879, during a congressional committee hearing, Sherman exhorted: "It will be a grave error if by negligence we permit the military law to become emasculated by allowing lawyers to interject into it the principles derived from their practice in the civil courts."[13] This more authoritarian viewpoint of military law expressed by General Sherman had early origins. For example, during debate on the 1806 Articles of War, Congressman Benjamin Tallmadge of Connecticut, after speaking in support of an amendment that would allow soldiers convicted of mutiny to be executed, reminded his colleagues that during the Revolutionary War officers had been threatened by mutiny on various occasions. Tallmadge warned that soldiers "were a description of men that must be ruled with severity."[14] In a similar fashion, in 1879 General Sherman reminded the congressional committee: "The object of military law is to govern armies composed of strong men. . . . An Army is a collection of armed men obliged to obey one man. . . . All the traditions of civil lawyers are antagonistic to this vital principle."[15] In that same year, G. Norman Lieber, the judge advocate general who was to review Kid's court-martial and who shared some of Sherman's views, argued that "Military Law is founded on the idea of a departure from civil law, and it seems to me a grave error to suffer it to become a sacrifice to principles of civil jurisprudence at variance with its objects."[16] It should not be surprising that some judge advocate generals shared Sherman's view that the commander in the field held supreme power over his men.

In 1878 Congress added section 1199, a new statute that authorized that the "Judge Advocate-General shall receive, revise, and have recorded the proceedings of all courts-martial." Some believed that this transformed the Judge Advocate General's Department into an appeals court. Lieber disagreed and took a more conservative view that "the power of revision did not exist in section 1199."[17] In other words, the Judge Advocate General's Department had no authority actually to revise courts-martial.

It is apparent that during the nineteenth century most U.S. Army officers subscribed to an authoritarian, paternalistic version of military law, and some considered Winthrop's views heretical. There is some evidence of friction between Lieber and Winthrop at the Judge Advocate General's Department.[18] Although reviled by some, Winthrop's *Military Law and Precedents* "became the classic work on American military law" and has been consulted by courts-martial panels, judge advocates, and defense counsels alike.[19]

Throughout the nineteenth century this debate on the application of military law raged; the moderates led by Winthrop and other judge advocate generals called for providing more protections for the defendant, while conservatives advocated strong discipline and harsh punishment. Winthrop strongly encouraged military laws that would grant full rights that the U.S. Constitution provided for defendants in civilian courts. For example, Winthrop lamented that the defendant in a court-martial "had a privilege to have counsel present, but it did not include permission to speak!"[20] Colonel Winthrop thought it was humiliating to allow counsel to be present yet not be allowed to speak in defense of his client. This rule was commonly used against civil lawyers but not the military officers who defended soldiers during courts-martial. The powers of the commanding officer were pervasive in military jurisprudence because he had the authority to order a court-martial and to appoint officers of his choosing to the panel. Finally, he administered the court-martial and reviewed the decision and sentence of the trial panel. It was not so much whether the defendant was guilty, but what punishment should be administered.

Kid's court-martial occurred during a period in which the military justice system was in a state of flux; consequently, his case helps to illuminate the difficult conditions under which defense lawyers worked. Kid faced a court-martial panel that most likely concurred with Sherman's view that this type of proceeding was meant to administer punishment—no more, no less.

A military court-martial, unlike a federal court, was not part of the federal judiciary of the United States and was not regulated by any inferior court established by Congress. Since courts-martial were not part of the judiciary branch, they were under the control of the President as commander-in-chief. Consequently, a court-martial was not really a court, and there was no English common law precedent to observe. Courts-martial, unlike superior courts, had no fixed place to meet and hold sessions and no permanent office or court's clerk. Therefore, they were not "courts of record." Any judgments or sentences ordered by court-martial could not be appealed to any civil court. Nevertheless, military law still fell under the review of the U.S. Supreme Court. In *Dynes v. Hoover* (1857) the U.S. Supreme Court ruled that a court-martial was "altogether beyond the jurisdiction or inquiry of any civil tribunal whatever."[21] Nevertheless, some cases were heard, and the most common way for a subject of a court-martial to gain access to the federal courts was through a writ of *habeas corpus.* In general, during the nineteenth century the U.S. Supreme Court and inferior federal courts seldom dealt with cases involving courts-martial; when they did, they commonly involved civilians who had been tried under military law.[22] Finally, It seems clear that courts-martial were examples of what Winthrop would label summary justice, a concept espoused by advocates of the Sherman school of legal thinking; they were strictly criminal courts where final judgment could be only acquittal or a criminal sentence. The only real appeal from a court-martial that sentenced the defendant to death was to the President, who normally requested advice from the judge advocate general of the U.S. Army before making a final decision. Because the court-martial was a tribunal under the control of the executive branch, the appeal was to a superior executive authority.[23]

The constitutional rights of a defendant under military law differed from those of civilians being charged under the jurisdiction of a civil court. For example, the Fifth Amendment provided citizens being charged with a criminal offense with the right to an indictment from a grand jury "except in cases arising in the land or naval forces." The grand jury was a concept employed under the judicial branch of government and was not applicable to military defendants. Winthrop noted that the Fifth Amendment clearly distinguished "the military from the civil class as separate communities." Under the Sixth Amendment the civilian defendant had the right "to have the assistance of counsel for his defense," while under military law, according to Winthrop, it was not a right but only a privilege. Under this same amendment the defendant received the right "to be confronted with the witnesses against him," but not under military law. The Seventh Amendment protections against "excessive fines" and "cruel and unusual punishment" also did not apply under military law; however, they normally were observed as a general rule of practice.[24] Although a writ of *habeas corpus* might be issued by a court to any prisoner who claimed that he was being illegally detained, he could not be discharged under a courts-martial sentence "if the court had jurisdiction to try the offender."[25] As indicated, a military defendant received some of the protection of the U.S. Constitution, but with limitations.

Because there are such significant differences between the practices of a civil court and a military court, background material is in order to make courts-martial procedures understandable. Article 64 of the 1874 revised Articles of War provided authority for convening a general court-martial. All officers and soldiers in the U.S. Army were covered by the Articles of War and were subject to trial by court-martial for any violations. Usually the commanding officer who ordered the general court-martial established a place and time for the panel members to convene. He designated and assigned the panel members, the judge advocate, and the defense counsel. Panel members were listed by rank, with the highest ranking officer acting as the president. At least five members were required to convene a court-martial, and thirteen were preferred. The officers assembled in full uniform. Once a quorum had been assembled, the panel members, led by the presiding officer, entered the room and sat at a table on both sides of the president according to rank. The judge advocate and the defendant with his counsel sat at tables facing the panel. At this point the president opened the proceedings. They were open to the public and closed only when the room was cleared for deliberation. During any panel deliberation on legal issues the judge advocate, defendant and counsel, and the public were ordered out of the room while the panel made its ruling. Reporters were allowed to attend but on occasion were forbidden to take notes. Each member of the tribunal and defense counsel received a copy of the charges against the defendant. An enlisted man held in detention for court-martial was brought in by the officer of the guard. It was normal policy that the defendant not be handcuffed or shackled. At that point, defense counsel was introduced to the court. After the judge advocate read the charges against the defendant, defense counsel made a plea and the proceedings began.[26]

The judge advocate performed legal duties similar to those of a prosecutor in civilian law. The qualifications sought included proper training for the position and an absence of prejudice for or against the accused. The judge advocate was required to present the accused with copies of the charges and convening order and to request a list of witnesses needed to testify at the court-martial proceedings. Normally, he appointed a reporter to keep complete, accurate notes and secured clerks, orderlies, and interpreters to help him properly conduct the legal proceedings. In essence the judge advocate acted as prosecutor, yet he was also required to be the adviser to the court. While serving as the prosecutor he was authorized to conduct the prosecution to his best advantage. Nevertheless, the judge advocate was not simply the prosecutor but also a minister of justice. If there was no defense counsel, he was required to assist the accused in making his defense. In his capacity as the court recorder he was required to develop a report in writing of the entire proceedings of the court. This record included the orders by the commander convening the court, a list of the members of the military panel, and the full testimony. After the proceedings ended, the judge advocate forwarded the full record directly to the commanding officer who had ordered the court-martial.[27] It is interesting to note that during the nineteenth century, unlike military courts, most civilian courts that tried defendants for criminal charges were not required to keep a full copy of the proceedings. Murder trials on appeal were the exception and required that a full transcript be submitted to the reviewing authority. In other words, courts-martial records were complete regardless of the circumstances.

The Articles of War provided the prisoner and defense counsel with the right to challenge any members of a court-martial for cause stated openly to the court, and the panel of officers had the power to determine the relevancy and validity of all challenges. This article did not appear in either the British Articles of War or any early American version until enacted by Congress in 1806.[28] Apparently, this article and other modifications were made in order to make military law conform more closely with the U.S. Constitution. In some ways it resembled the *voir dire* practiced in civilian law that was controlled by the presiding judge. The *voir dire* allowed both defense and prosecution to question the prospective jurors to determine if they knew the defendant and to ascertain whether they had predetermined the defendant's guilt or innocence. Challenge of court members was one of the few real protections of the defendant's legal rights. Normally challenges were made after the specifications of charges were read to the accused and the names of the court members were revealed by the judge advocate. At that time the defense counsel was allowed to present any objections that he believed existed. Challenges were not treated as part of the courts-martial proceedings; instead, they were kept separate and examined during the review process.[29]

Only commissioned officers were permitted to serve on the court-martial panel. Considering that the challenge procedure could cause the diminution of court members, the commanding officer ordering the court-martial usually tried to appoint the higher number of officers to the panel. Nevertheless, five court members were sufficient. In the case under discussion General Nelson Miles appointed additional officers to his original panel to assure a quorum.

The main function of the panel's president was to keep order and to conduct the court's business in a fair manner. The president had the authority to speak for the court in every instance in which a rule of action had been prescribed by law or regulations. The president opened the proceedings and called the court to order and also announced the adjournment at the close of the session. He had to be sure that the rights of everyone involved were respected. When the panel was ready to deliberate on any legal issue, he ordered the courtroom to be cleared of all others present. After a vote had been taken, he reconvened the court and announced the decision of the court panel. He lacked authority to announce rulings or make decisions independently of the panel. All communications conducted between the court and the commanding officer who ordered the court-martial were made by the presiding officer. The hierarchical, authoritarian nature of the military, the esprit de corps, and the characteristics of military group solidarity that permeated the military court added a unique flavor—a flavor that very much influenced the outcome of Kid's court-martial.[30]

Each panel member had an equal vote, and all issues and questions had to be decided by a majority vote. All panel members had to vote on every issue, and the order of voting began with the youngest officer in commission. This procedure was used to assure that junior officers were not unduly influenced by the views of senior officers. The ineffectiveness of the requirement must have been obvious during the panel discussions throughout Kid's court-martial. In an authoritarian setting and such a restricted venue as Kid's trial, younger officers had to know how their senior officers would vote. They knew the consequences if they resisted the wishes of their superiors. Whatever their beliefs or opinions, all of the panel members knew that they had to act as a unit and that all court members were prohibited from disclosing their vote or making their views public. Consequently, in a military court all dissent was eliminated in the final decision reached by the panel members. No member of the court was permitted to record or openly protest a ruling or judgment of the majority.[31] This concept of unanimity and the inability to discuss the final judgment has no parallel in civilian law, in which, after trials are concluded, jurors talk about the process and their feelings about the defendant, defense counsel, and prosecutor. It goes to the core of military logic that during courts-martial the main purpose was to enforce discipline within the ranks. The finality of a court-martial was assured by the "closing of the ranks" of the officers on the panel and in their decision to act as one voice. They subscribed to the "principle that all military action must . . . be summary, final and conclusive."[32] In the end it was a military action, hierarchical and open to question only by those higher in authority, such as the commanding officer who ordered the proceedings. Some might argue that in this type of military environment any real "search for the truth" would be impossible.

The judge advocate introduced the witnesses, who were required to take an oath before testifying. Chinese witnesses were sworn under the usual form of oath administered through an interpreter, who would explain the pledge to the witness. Indian witnesses were usually sworn in a similar fashion. Witnesses were subject to cross-examination by defense counsel.[33] Any member of the court was allowed to question witnesses. The accused was to be accorded every legal right and was not to be embarrassed or placed at a disadvantage. All officers and enlisted men were presumed to have some knowledge of the laws and regulations governing the army, but enlisted men recruited from the ranks of recently arrived immigrants or Indians usually had a limited knowledge of the Articles of War. Officers were required to read and explain all of the articles to every enlisted man in their command.[34] Since there were 128 complex articles, it should not be surprising to learn that officers seldom complied with this requirement.

The results of a general court-martial were reviewed by the commanding officer who had ordered that charges be made against the accused. He could either approve or disapprove the proceedings or sentence, and he had the right to pardon or mitigate the punishment recommended by the court-martial panel. All sentences or proceedings had to be approved by the commanding officer. If he refused to approve the sentence, he returned the transcript of the proceedings and ordered the panel to reassemble and reconsider their findings. He detailed the issues within the findings and sentence that he viewed as problematic. At that point the full panel met again, resumed deliberations, and made the suggested corrections.

Pardon or mitigation was common with a defendant who was a young and inexperienced recruit or someone with little understanding of the English language. When returning the court-martial proceedings with his formal action, the commander added his reflections upon the conclusions reached by the court, the conduct of the prosecution or defense, the final record, or other factors he deemed appropriate.[35] Although the commander held tremendous power under military law, he realized that he would be held accountable. He could be overruled by the judge advocate general, the secretary of war, or the President of the United States.[36] After the final proceedings were amended and approved by the commanding officer, the full record was forwarded directly to the Judge Advocate General's Department in Washington,

D.C.; consequently, the archives of general courts-martial are extensive and complete.

Despite modest changes in the Articles of War, U.S. Army commanders continued to dominate trials by court-martial. For example, in 1919, in an address before a bar association luncheon, John Henry Wigmore, a former judge advocate speaking on military justice, explained that the military system "knows what it wants; and it systematically goes in and gets it." Wigmore reflected General Sherman's earlier comments by stating, "Military justice wants *discipline*—that is, action in obedience to regulations and orders; this being absolutely necessary for prompt, competent, and decisive handling of masses of men."[37] There were, however, a few astute critics of such conservative military thinking. During congressional hearings at the end of World War I, Acting Judge Advocate General Samuel T. Ansell became involved in a sharp debate with General Enoch H. Crowder on modifying the Articles of War.[38] Reflecting the earlier complaints of Winthrop about the lack of legal rights accorded military defendants, Ansell believed that major changes needed to be made to bring the Articles of War into line with the U.S. Constitution. Crowder, on the other hand, supported the views of Sherman, as did many others. In an impassioned plea Ansell claimed "that the existing system of Military Justice is un-American . . . that it is archaic . . . and regulated by the mere power of Military Command rather than Law."[39] Despite a spirited debate and sharp criticism, virtually all of Ansell's suggested changes were excluded from the new military code. Yale law professor Edmund M. Morgan, who had served as assistant to the judge advocate general during the war and supported Ansell's liberal changes in the Articles of War, lamented that "the military theory prevails and will continue to prevail until changed by legislation."[40] As noted earlier, during the nineteenth century most U.S. Army officers subscribed to a more authoritarian, paternalistic version of military law; they were more concerned with discipline and punishment than justice, and that had not changed in the twentieth century.

This sharp debate resurfaced right after World War II when Congress held five weeks of hearings before enacting the *Uniform Code of Military Justice* (UCMJ). Ironically, Edmund Morgan chaired the committee to rewrite the Articles of War. Once again, a sharp, sometimes acrimonious debate occurred, in which Colonel Frederick B. Wiener best reflected the continuing dominance of the conservative view of military law. In his extensive testimony before the committee Wiener recited General Sherman's earlier objections against incorporating any ideas of civil law into a new military code. Wiener claimed that "there is a lot of silly, loose talk about the system of military justice being un-American" and that such talk indicated "the ignorance of the speaker" making such claims. Wiener was, of course, criticizing Ansell's earlier statement that still had support, including that of Morgan. Wiener opposed the more liberal version of the bill, claiming that it would "prevent the military commander from influencing the court."[41] After five weeks of spirited debate, Congress accepted a conservative version of the *Uniform Code of Military Justice* that reflected Colonel Wiener's recommendations. Edward F. Sherman claimed that "the UCMJ, as enacted, was a compromise which left commanders in control of court-martial" procedures.[42]

In 1956, U.S. Supreme Court Justice Hugo L. Black in a legal opinion observed that "traditionally, military justice has been a rough form of justice emphasizing summary procedures, speedy convictions and stern penalties with a view of maintaining obedience. . . . There has always been less emphasis in the military on protecting the rights of the individual than in civilian society and civilian courts."[43] Three years later Justice William O. Douglas commented that "the military trial is marked by the age-old manifest destiny of retributive justice."[44] Conservatives argued that desertion and insubordination, although not crimes in civilian life, were such that the very existence of an army depended upon their deterrence for self-preservation.[45] In September 2000, reflecting General Sherman's philosophy, John S. Cooke, a former judge advocate and noted military legal scholar, claimed that "protections of civilian criminal justice, and protecting the rights of the individual was not a primary purpose of the system." He argued that military law relied heavily on deterrence and punishment that, it was hoped, would be administered by a commander with a high sense of honor, character, and legal knowledge that would enable him to assure justice for the defendant. Cooke concluded that reformers such as Winthrop and other judge advocate generals focused their activities mainly on codifying and explaining military law, a process that would help to standardize legal procedures and their applications during courts-martial proceedings.[46] Although it might be considered a very modest attempt to change the system, Winthrop's treatise provided the basic knowledge for judge advocates, defense counsels, and commanders to comply with rules of military law as practiced throughout the U.S. Army.

Winthrop's *Military Law and Precedents* remained the premier book on military law and was reprinted in 1920 and 1942. It has been consulted often because it illuminated and explained the basic legal procedures for conducting a court-martial. Winthrop's comprehensive legal citations and documentation are quite remarkable. His influence has helped to bring about change, including legal counsel and their right to speak for defendants during courts-martial.[47] It has become the authoritative volume on military law consulted by legal scholars throughout the twentieth century. Such famous jurists as Melville Fuller, Hugo Black, Harlan Fiske Stone, and Stanley Reed, all members of the U.S. Supreme Court, quoted it in their opinions from 1900 through 1955.[48] In 2006, in *Hamdan v. Rumsfeld, Secretary of Defense, et al.*, a case involving the detention of "terrorists" at Guantanamo, lawyers and jurists cited Winthrop. U.S. Supreme Court Justice John Paul Stevens observed: "The classic treatise penned by Colonel William Winthrop, whom we have called the 'Blackstone of Military Law' . . . describes at least four preconditions for exercise of jurisdiction by a tribunal of the type convened to try Hamdan." During the arguments in this landmark case, Winthrop's treatise on military law was cited extensively. The U.S.

Supreme Court ruled in favor of Hamdan.[49] It is a remarkable tribute to a judge advocate general who fought valiantly to provide justice for all soldiers brought before a general court-martial panel.

Desertion and mutiny are the two concerns in this discussion about Kid and military law. The Articles of War of 1874 bestowed harsh punishment on deserters and mutineers. Article 32 provided provisions for punishing any soldier who left his duty station without leave from his commanding officer. Those who violated this article would be what was commonly called absent without leave, or AWOL.[50] Any soldier who failed to return to his duty station for an extended period of time would be presumed to be a deserter and could be punished by a court-martial. In order for military authorities to substantiate a charge of desertion, they were required to establish that the person was absent without authority and that he left with no intention of returning to his unit. Mitigating circumstances affecting a charge of desertion might include being "under the influence of liquor" and returning voluntarily after a brief absence. The person who was AWOL had to return of his own free will, not by capture. Military commanders might also show leniency if the deserter was "young and inexperienced" or if his commanding officer had never explained the Articles of War, which would prevent his comprehending the gravity of the offense. Punishment for desertion was within the discretion of the court to decide. In times of war deserters could be severely punished.[51]

Under Article 22, mutiny was defined as the actions of any soldier who excited, caused, or joined in any mutiny or sedition with the intention of subverting the authority of any superior military officer. The intent might be openly declared or implied by actions that might lead to "subversion or suppression" of a commanding officer. Actions of this kind could include taking weapons and exhibiting a menacing attitude toward an officer. Any soldier convicted of mutiny "shall suffer death, or such other punishment as a court-martial may direct." Article 23 declared that a soldier present at a mutiny who failed to warn his commanding officer of such actions or who failed to suppress a mutiny would suffer the same penalty as those convicted of mutiny. Military authorities had developed rules to deal harshly with deserters and mutineers, especially during times of war; however, they failed to explain them adequately to the enlisted men.[52]

Kid had been charged with two crimes listed in the Articles of War: desertion and mutiny. If he was convicted of these serious charges he could receive the death sentence. By being absent without leave from his military duty station to follow Apache social traditions, Kid was about to be rudely introduced to U.S. military law.

COURT-MARTIAL

I killed only one man whose name is "Rip" because he killed my
grandfather. I am not educated like you and therefore can't say very
much. . . . That is all I have to say.

FIRST SERGEANT KID, General Court Martial
Records, 117, December 27, 1887

·   ·   ·

The court-martial of First Sergeant Kid, Company A Indian Scouts at
San Carlos, convened June 28, 1887, with all members of the panel
and the judge advocate present. General Nelson A. Miles had appointed
Second Lieutenant Laurence Davis Tyson, a West Point graduate, class
of 1883, to serve as the judge advocate. Tyson's first action was to accept
First Lieutenant John Arthur Baldwin as counsel for the accused and
Robert McIntosh and Shago as interpreters to the court. A West Point
graduate and a graduate of the Infantry and Cavalry School (1885),
Lieutenant Baldwin had been appointed by General Miles as defense
counsel because of his experience in handling legal cases.[1]

After he received his orders Baldwin had requested that he be allowed
to withdraw as defense counsel in several other legal cases at Fort
Thomas. Baldwin advised his commander that he had received a
telegram from General Miles ordering him to serve as counsel in the
Indian scout cases to be tried by courts-martial at San Carlos. His com-

mander granted Baldwin's request, and since Baldwin was appointed on short notice he had to hand over his current legal cases quickly, probably left rather abruptly, and spent a full day traveling the thirty miles from Fort Thomas to San Carlos. This gave him less than two days to make his trip and to prepare his defense. This no doubt increased the pressure on Baldwin, who would have little time to interview his Apache clients to determine the facts of the case and how to make a strong defense. Baldwin had received a very difficult assignment complicated because his clients were Apaches; the language barrier in itself created a Gordian knot. Baldwin was at a decided disadvantage and found it difficult to prepare adequately to defend Kid; nevertheless, during the court-martial he was to prove that he had been the right choice for the job.

General Miles selected Baldwin to defend Kid and his four scouts for several reasons. First, Baldwin's expertise in military law made him a skilled defense lawyer. Second, he was a Military Academy graduate who most likely had received instruction on military law from Judge Advocate General G. Norman Lieber at West Point. Finally, there seems little doubt that Baldwin subscribed to Colonel Winthrop's theory of military law that advocated providing full rights for all defendants in a court-martial. Miles must have realized that Baldwin would provide a strong defense for Kid, and the commander also knew that the members of the court-martial panel he selected would harbor strong bias against the Apache defendants. General Miles understood that the mutiny charges against Kid and his scouts would be taken seriously by virtually every army officer in Arizona Territory, and no doubt they expected these rebellious Indians to be punished severely. Fresh in their minds was the Cibecue mutiny, which had cost the lives of one officer and six enlisted men only six years earlier.

On June 29, 1887, Judge Advocate Tyson, acting as the prosecutor, filed two charges against Kid. First, the scout was accused of mutiny, in violation of Article 22, by disobeying Captain Pierce's order to go to the guardhouse. Mutiny is defined as "an unlawful opposition or resistance to, or defiance of superior military authority, with a deliberate purpose to usurp, subvert, or override the same."[2] The act of mutiny could be declared openly or could result in the hostile actions of the accused, such as subverting the superior authority. Such actions might be demonstrated through using arms to resist any superior authority.[3] Any soldier convicted of mutiny usually suffered the highest consequence, a death sentence. The judge advocate also charged Kid with desertion. According to the charge, on June 1, 1887, the defendant had deserted and fled from San Carlos and had not returned until June 25, 1887. Although not as severe as mutiny, desertion is often dealt with harshly. In Kid's case, because he had not been instructed in the Articles of War, defense counsel could plead ignorance of the law as a mitigating factor. There were at least five precedents in which this legal concept had been applied as a mitigating factor in the final decision on punishment.[4] Equally important, the punishment of a deserter is within "the discretion of the court" to decide. After hearing the specific charges filed against Kid, Baldwin pleaded his client not guilty on both counts. Further, he argued that since the defendant had returned to his post and surrendered voluntarily, the charge of desertion was not correct. With the filing of the charges against Kid, the court-martial could now proceed.[5]

Only thirty-five years old, Baldwin had superb credentials: he had attended West Point, had received his commission in 1872, and was attached to the Ninth Infantry, where his duty included defending officers and enlisted men under courts-martial. He had about one day to prepare his case before the court-martial was convened. Did he actually interview Kid before the court-martial? If so, did he have enough time to get all the facts about the case and what his client would say if he made a statement to the court? Naturally, whatever he may have learned about Kid's version of the mutiny would be filtered through two interpreters. We do not know what Baldwin knew about Apaches or any other Indians, but it is doubtful that he had ever defended one in a court-martial before, because cases involving scouts were rare. His defense of Kid seems to fit into a pattern of trials in which Indians were tried for major crimes in Arizona and California.[6] Baldwin would have difficulty effectively defending Indian defendants. The language translation problem was difficult enough, let alone actually understanding enough Apache culture to use it in a defense. Nevertheless, Baldwin proved to be a strong advocate for Kid.

On July 2, 1887, Judge Advocate Tyson reconvened the court-martial for further deliberations and, over the challenge of defense counsel Baldwin, seated as panel members Major Anson Mills, Lieutenant L. P. Hunt, and Lieutenant R. L. Read, all attached to the Tenth Cavalry. With six of the eight members of the court panel West Point graduates, as well as Judge Advocate Tyson and defense counsel Baldwin, it was a well-trained group of officers, who most likely were rule-conscious.[7]

Some of the officers selected by General Miles had considerable military experience and were well versed in court-martial proceedings. Major Mills, president of the panel, had received an appointment to the U.S. Military Academy from Texas on July 1, 1855. He had extensive service during the Civil War and was cited for gallantry in the battles at Murfreesboro, Tennessee; Chickamauga, Georgia; and Nashville, Tennessee, and in the battle at Slim Buttes, Montana, on September 9, 1876. In July and August 1864, during the Civil War, Major Mills had captured 350 rebel troops trying to retreat. He experienced varied service in the American West and served under the command of Colonel Henry Carrington and Captain William J. Fetterman, who were known for their engagements with Red Cloud's Sioux at Fort Kearney. Mills received promotions quickly and had been advanced to the rank of major in April 1878.[8]

Another panel member, First Lieutenant Hayden DeLany, had received gallantry citations on May 1, 1868, for action against the Paiute Indians in Warner Valley, Oregon, and for action against Indians on the Big Horn in Montana on November 25, 1876. Most of the others on the panel were regular army officers with experience in the Indian wars. Lieutenants William G. Elliot; James Bryan Hughes; Robert Doddridge Read, Jr.; and Levi Pettibone Hunt also were West Point graduates.[9] Captain Robert Geno Smither and Lieutenant Carter H. Johnson,

Tenth Cavalry, were the exceptions to the rule. They both had begun their military service as enlisted men and eventually received commissions. Promoted to lieutenant in 1882, Johnson had received a transfer to the Tenth Cavalry, stationed at Fort Thomas. After Baldwin completed a series of challenges to members of the courts-martial panel (to be discussed in chapter 5), the proceedings began.[10]

In order to re-create and analyze the events during the alleged mutiny on June 1, 1887, it is important to set the physical scene that surrounded Al Sieber's tent. The San Carlos Agency buildings were situated on a flat, sprawling plain about forty-five feet above the Gila River. The guardhouse and the trader's store were situated about 135 yards north of the agency buildings, and the long lines of soldiers' white tents were about 400 yards further north. The officers' tents were approximately 100 yards from Sieber's tent. The Apache scouts lived in a group of wickiups, dwellings constructed of brush, situated between the guardhouse and the officers' tents. The school buildings were on the east side overlooking the San Carlos River, which flowed into the Gila River.

At about 5:00 p.m. Captain Francis E. Pierce and Al Sieber were standing in front of Sieber's tent when Kid, accompanied by Askisaylala, Bachoandoth, Margey, and Nahconquisay, the four scouts under his command, arrived to surrender. Kid and his four scouts were standing facing Captain Pierce and Sieber, with one or more chairs between them. Gonshayee and about eleven of Kid's SI band members, some armed with rifles and ammunition belts, were on horseback behind them, intently watching the five scouts as they prepared to surrender. Captain Alpheus Bowman, standing about a hundred yards away in the officers' tent row, became curious and decided to walk over to witness what was happening. Pierce had called for Antonio Díaz and Frederick Knipple to attend the surrender to act as interpreters from Apache to Spanish to English and back. This complicated method of interpreting the Apache dialect often created problems in understanding exactly what was being

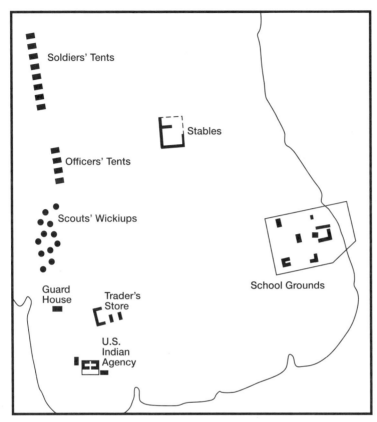

Old San Carlos Agency, Arizona, in the 1890s. Courtesy Melodie Tune,
graphic artist, Instructional Technology Services, San Diego State University

said and understood by all parties involved. The use of Antonio Díaz to interpret from Apache to Spanish also proved to be problematic. Díaz apparently held some animosity toward Kid, and under such circumstances it would not be surprising that Díaz might have made mistakes, intentional or otherwise, in interpreting what Kid actually said. No doubt the testimony of the Apache witnesses was influenced by the use of two translators.

After the court-martial convened, the judge advocate called Captain Pierce, the Indian agent, as the first witness. Pierce stated that he had known Kid for about two years and that the scout had reenlisted in April 1887 with Captain P. L. Lee's company of Apache scouts. Captain Pierce testified that on June 1, 1887, Gonshayee, acting as a messenger, came to San Carlos and informed him that Kid wanted to talk to him. Pierce: "I told him that he could come if he pleased and that the sooner he came the better it would be for him."[11] Kid had been absent without leave several days and had ridden to Aravaipa Canyon, where he had killed Rip in retribution for murdering his grandfather. Captain Pierce was not interested in that shooting; it was Kid's leaving his duty station and being away without leave for five days that had upset the captain. Pierce testified that Kid and the four scouts came in about sundown and were waiting for him in front of Sieber's tent. Captain Pierce and Sieber walked over to meet with Kid, and Pierce asked him: "Where are the five scouts who have been absent. They all stepped to the front in a line. I said 'Kid give me your rifle.' He handed it to me and I said 'give me your belt,' he handed it to me." Then Pierce ordered the scouts to go to the "calaboose," meaning the guardhouse. Antonio Díaz, acting as the interpreter for Pierce, explained to the scouts what they were required to do. Pierce remembered: "Just then I heard a little noise that attracted my attention in front of the tent and I saw a few men on horseback who were bringing down their fire arms and getting cartridges from their belts. I said 'lookout Sieber they are going to fire.' Immediately there was a shot fired by some one in the party in front of the tent." According to Pierce, "There were about fifteen to twenty-five shots fired" into Sieber's tent, and the chief of scouts took a bullet in the ankle. The five scouts fled south on foot toward the Gila River, followed quickly by Gonshayee and fellow San Carlos SI band members, some of whom had fired shots at Sieber.[12] The fifteen or twenty shots, by which only Sieber was hit once, might lead one to believe that the Apaches were poor shots. At that distance it would have been hard to miss with rifles. It seems logical to conclude that they were only trying to scare Sieber and Captain Pierce in order to allow the scouts to escape.

Judge Advocate Tyson wanted to convince the panel that Kid was an important member of the SI band with enough influence to lead his scouts to mutiny. When asked about Kid's authority, Pierce explained that after Kid's grandfather, Togodechuz, chief of the band, had been killed the previous December, another man had been selected by the band as chief. Referring to Kid's being held in high regard by SI band members, Pierce testified that Kid's "name was mentioned as successor to his grandfather," but they selected Gonshayee. During cross-examination Lieutenant Baldwin asked: "Was he [Kid] the popular choice for chief of his people?" Pierce responded, "He was not the popular choice." Asked by Tyson whether he had considerable influence with his band, Pierce replied, "I think he has considerable influence in his band." In other words, Tyson was trying to demonstrate that Kid, with strong authority over his scouts, was a dangerous threat to the established military authority at San Carlos. No doubt this sort of logic appealed to the officers on the panel, who displayed strong group solidarity, a band of brothers. Then Tyson asked how long Kid had been absent from his post, and Pierce replied, "twenty-five days." Even though Kid returned voluntarily, this information helped to affirm the charge of desertion.[13] It is important to note, however, that the word "mutiny" only appears twice in the testimony: Baldwin used the phrases "alleged mutiny" and "supposed mutiny" during his cross-examination of Captain Pierce.[14] It may be that mutiny was implied and therefore understood by the panel. Consequently, Tyson felt that it was unnecessary to discuss it. As noted earlier, members of the panel probably had the disastrous 1881 Cibecue mutiny on their minds, yet they never stated it openly during the court-martial.

During cross-examination Baldwin asked Pierce who had acted as the medium of communication with Kid. Pierce replied: "Gonshayee." Asked about the number of Indians in front of Sieber's tent, Pierce acknowledged that there were about twenty, most of them on horseback. Pierce admitted that Kid had handed in his arms as requested. Baldwin: "Did you see the accused take his arms or any arms?" Pierce: "I did not." Baldwin: "Did you see or hear the accused do a hostile act,

either by word, look, or movement?" Pierce: "I did not." Defense counsel asked to whom he was referring when stating they were "going to
fire." Pierce replied, to the Apaches "who were on horseback, men of his
band." According to Pierce the first shot came from the center of the
mounted horsemen. Asked where Kid was standing when the shooting
began, Pierce said: "He was standing close to the chair that I had put
the belts on, and close to Sieber and myself." Pierce testified that several
"shots came almost all together after the first one." Baldwin: "Did the
accused have time to obey your directions to go to the calaboose?"
Pierce: "He did not have time to go. He had time to start, I supposed he
was going, he appeared to be making preparations." Baldwin asked
Pierce if he called upon the accused to suppress the riot or revolt.
Pierce: "I did not."[15]

Then Baldwin asked a very important question. Had any officer
instructed Kid "in the rules and articles of war?" Pierce replied, "The
articles of war have never been read and translated to him to my knowledge. He has been verbally instructed in his duties as a soldier." This, of
course, is a critical issue, because the Articles of War demanded that all
enlisted men and officers receive training on these rules. Pierce testified
that, as the Indian agent at San Carlos, he was in charge of controlling
the Indian police. A member of the court-martial panel asked, "Is
Gonshayee a man of strong personal influence among his people?" After
objections by defense counsel the judge advocate ordered the witness to
answer the question. Pierce, "I do not think he is. He has complained to
me several times that he could not do any thing with them. That they
would not obey him."[16] This last question reiterated the belief by some
that Kid had greater influence in the SI band than Gonshayee, who
apparently had been the second choice of his fellow band members.
Although selected band chief, Gonshayee not only lacked good character
and judgment but also appeared to be a somewhat sinister character who
exhibited poor leadership qualities. As noted earlier, Gonshayee may
have been jealous of Kid's popularity in the SI band and resentful that he
had not been considered first for chief; consequently, he may have

goaded Kid into taking action against Rip at an inopportune time while Kid was serving in the army and under military law.

Al Sieber, a civilian employed by the U.S. Army as chief of scouts, was sworn in as the prosecution's second witness in his quarters because he had been recovering from a gunshot wound in the foot. Sieber, born February 29, 1844, in Germany, had emigrated to the United States, had served in the Civil War, and eventually had ended up in Arizona Territory about 1868. He served briefly as a scout under General George Stoneman and in 1871 worked as a guide for Colonel Julius Mason while in pursuit of hostiles near Prescott. In the following year, with the arrival of General George Crook in Arizona, Sieber enlisted as a scout and was given command of Apache scouts. According to various sources Sieber

Al Sieber, chief of scouts, 1887. Courtesy Arizona State Library, Archives and Public Records, History and Archives Division, Phoenix, #97-8428

had suffered up to twenty-nine wounds from bullets and arrows. Sieber received an appointment as chief of Apache scouts in 1882 and continued to hold that position until 1885.

Called as a witness by the judge advocate, Sieber testified that on June 1, 1887, Kid had been absent without leave for five days before he returned to San Carlos about five in the evening. In front of his tent, Sieber pointed out the five scouts who had been absent without leave, and Pierce disarmed them. Asked what happened next, Sieber replied, "Kid being the nearest to me made a grab for his carbine which I grabbed with my right hand and shoved Kid back with my left."[17] This may be the most crucial statement in the entire court-martial, and it contradicted Pierce's testimony. Since Sieber was in a great deal of pain, he might have been confused about exactly what happened. Sieber testified that Captain Pierce shouted, "Look out Sieber they are going to shoot." Sieber: "At this time there were two shots fired one right after the other, Kid jumped away from me and ran around" the tent. Sieber then ran into the tent to grab his gun. After retrieving his rifle Sieber ran out the front of the tent and took a shot at the first Apache he saw on horseback. This Apache apparently fired at the same time. During this exchange of shots Sieber received a severe gunshot wound in the ankle and fell back into his tent. Asked the identity of the Apaches who had accompanied Kid when he surrendered, Sieber replied, "They were Indians who belong to San Carlos 'I' band, Gonshayee Chief." Sieber said all of the scouts and Kid were members of Gonshayee's band. Questioned about the attitude of the SI band members who were watching the surrender, Sieber claimed, "My opinion as to their appearance is that it was war-like, I thought so by their looks, and by their having arms in their hands, which is against orders here." Asked if Kid started to head for the guardhouse, Sieber answered: "Yes, I thought that Kid did make a movement as though he wanted to go." Tyson asked Sieber how he interpreted the look that Kid had given the other scouts. Sieber replied, "Kid gave the look to these four scouts. . . . I thought they had an understanding before they came in here, that if a certain thing transpired, which was ordering them to the guardhouse when they did come in, that by a look from Kid, each man, knew what to do, which they did in each man jumping for their arms."[18] Sieber testified that Kid was as prominent as any member in the SI band.

Once again, trying to counteract the attempts by the judge advocate to establish that Kid was the most influential member of the SI band, Baldwin stated: "I intend to show further on that for nearly nine years the accused has been a soldier of the United States. He has severed his tribal relations." Further, "You are trying a duly enlisted soldier, and not the accused as an Indian."[19] Was Kid an Indian or was he a soldier? It was a complex issue. Captain Pierce had already testified that Kid had not been trained in the Articles of War. Baldwin realized that Kid and his scouts drifted back and forth between two polar opposites, military and tribal. It becomes clear later in the court-martial that Baldwin understood this ambivalent life led by Kid and that Kid and his scouts were torn by two sets of rules. The scouts knew they were required to obey the captain, but their knowledge of the Articles of War had to be marginal. On the one hand, Baldwin knew that if Kid was a soldier and had influence over his scouts, it would probably lead the panel members to be convinced that the first sergeant of scouts indeed had led a mutiny outside Sieber's tent. On the other hand, since not a single member of the court panel had been removed by challenging, Baldwin probably accepted the fact that Tyson believed he had, to use a modern phrase, what would be called "a slam dunk" case. General Miles had ordered Kid tried as a soldier, but both Baldwin and Miles knew that this was unfair because of the transient nature of Apache scouts. Under such conditions, which do you choose: Kid as an Indian or as a soldier? Baldwin, no doubt, realized that he was between a rock and a hard place. Therefore, he probably believed it would be useless to argue about the amount of influence that Kid had over his band. At that point the court-martial panel adjourned because Sieber was in pain and was having difficulty testifying. The judge advocate waived the right to further examine Sieber on the direct examination.[20]

The judge advocate swore in Frederick Knipple, issue clerk, as his next witness. Knipple testified that Captain Pierce had summoned him to interpret from Spanish to English. Knipple testified that he knew Kid and that he had watched the group of mounted Apaches arrive. Knipple claimed that he saw Captain Pierce and Antonio Díaz come up to meet the scouts. Knipple noticed the five Apaches who were standing in front of Sieber's tent and he heard someone say look out, they are going to shoot. Knipple dashed into the tent as Sieber rushed outside to fire a shot. The clerk testified that he did not know the identity of the group of Apaches on horseback behind the scouts. During Baldwin's cross-examination, Knipple acknowledged that he became alarmed and excited by the shooting. Asked if he understood the Apache language, he answered: "No sir." Baldwin: "Are you positive you saw one Indian rush for his gun?" He replied: "Yes sir, I am." Asked the identity of the Indian who tried to grab the gun, he answered: "I don't know sir." Knipple admitted that since he was running for cover he did not actually see anyone shoot.[21]

Captain Alpheus H. Bowman, called to testify, acknowledged that as he watched the surrendering of arms he recognized Kid. Asked about the disturbance, he testified that he saw a group of Indians and walked over to observe them more closely. Bowman: "I noticed that they were armed,

San Carlos guardhouse and Indian Police, 1880. Apache defendants were incarcerated here before their trials. Courtesy Arizona State Library, Archives and Public Records, History and Archives Division, Phoenix, #95-2823

all had rifles except one person [Gonshayee] who was with a squaw."
After watching them for a few minutes Bowman returned to his own
tent, where he talked to Lieutenant Watson and several other officers
about these hostile-looking Apaches on horseback. After a brief conversation, he decided to return to Sieber's tent and watch the proceedings
more closely. Bowman testified: "I endeavored to get some information
from one of them. . . . I found the Indians uncommunicative and sullen
in their manner towards me and not disposed to talk." He admitted that
he was near the tent for "only a few moments when the firing began."
Bowman observed the Indians running away from Sieber's tent, and
some of them were firing at the tent.[22]

During cross-examination Baldwin asked, "Have you not expressed
bias and prejudice against the defendant when a member of this Court?"
Bowman responded, "Yes." He admitted again that he had not actually
seen "any individual Indian" fire at Sieber. Asked where he was standing
when he first saw Captain Pierce, Bowman responded: "I was in front of
my own tent a hundred yards away." Asked how many Indians on horseback were in front of Sieber's tent, Bowman replied, "I counted eleven."
Baldwin: "Did you believe at that time there was trouble brewing at that
tent?" Bowman testified, "No, I only thought that something unusual
was in the air." The judge advocate asked him if he communicated to the
commanding officer "any impressions made by the sullen manner" of
the Indians that he had seen that might have suggested a threat to Pierce
and Sieber. Bowman answered, "I made no communication to the
Commanding Officer for the double reason that I was not sufficiently
advised of Indian affairs to presume to make any suggestions or offer my
opinions about matters that related purely to Indian affairs." When
Baldwin asked him if he could speak or understand the Apache language, he replied, "No. I allude to speaking to them in my testimony.
The man I spoke to had a white hat on and was a very light complex-
ioned man; he . . . had the appearance of a boy who had been at school,
or a Mexican, and I spoke to him." Baldwin asked him if he was armed
when he returned to Sieber's tent to watch, and he replied no. Bowman

acknowledged that when he spoke to them, "They shook their heads and said: 'No sabe.'"[23] It is worth noting that Bowman, like Pierce, did not see the Apaches as a threat but believed that they were just watching the surrender. If he had considered them a danger he probably would have returned from his tent with a sidearm.

The judge advocate called William Duchin, a blacksmith, and, soon after, Charles S. Chew, who provided conflicting testimony on who was doing the shooting. Duchin testified that he saw the scouts arrive in front of Sieber's tent, and about fifteen minutes later he heard shooting. The witness said that he saw Kid run between the outhouse and the dormitory, where he stopped and fired a shot. Duchin testified that Kid "shot toward the sutler's store." Asked how far away he was from the defendant, Duchin replied that it was about a hundred yards. Asked if he saw anyone else shoot, he said John, a scout, standing by the hospital, fired at the renegades as they fled south toward the Gila River. When asked who else fired shots, he pointed to Kid. Judge advocate: "How far was the accused from the sutler's store when he did the firing mentioned?" Duchin: "I think it must be a thousand yards."[24] During cross-examination, Baldwin asked the witness to "point out the exact spot where the accused stood when he fired the shot you mention?" He could not point to the exact spot but suggested "it was somewhere between the outhouse and dormitory." Baldwin: "Did you see the face of the person, when the shot was fired?" Duchin: "No, I did not." Duchin claimed that it was Kid because he "recognized his gait, walk and face." Duchin's testimony was obviously contradictory. A member of the court, possibly confused by the testimony, asked, "Will you explain how it was that you could see a shot fired in the direction of the trader's store, and why you could not see the points indicated as being in the vicinity of the line of fire or why you could not see any one that may have been in the supposed line of fire?" Duchin: "The accused was right on the brow of the hill and I was below. I could see from the way he was pointing his gun the direction he was firing."[25] Duchin insisted that it was Kid who fired the shot. Other witnesses, including Pierce and Sieber, testified that Kid did not have a gun and that he fled from San Carlos without a weapon. That Duchin was unable to explain why he could not see the points on the line of fire suggests that he was either confused or lying about what he actually observed. It certainly reveals that his testimony was less than convincing, even to the panel member who asked the question.

Private Charles S. Chew, the second witness, admitted that he did not know Kid. Chew testified that he had been working at the quartermaster's office all day, and he heard and saw one man fire shots. When asked who fired the shot, he replied, "I could not tell. It was an Indian that fired it. It was right on the brow of this hill." He also testified that he was about sixty to seventy yards away from the Apache, who fired towards Sieber's tent. After firing the shot the Apache headed south and passed between the two corrals heading for the Gila River. When asked again about who fired the shot, whether it was a scout, he admitted that he could not distinguish scouts from the other Apaches. During cross-examination Baldwin asked, "Where did the Indians who passed in front of the officers' tents go?" Chew: "They all went over the hill." The witness further testified that the person who fired the shot "was mounted" on a horse.[26] It should be noted that earlier testimony by several witnesses verified that Kid and his four scouts were on foot. Obviously Kid did not fire the shot. It probably was one of the mounted SI band members who had witnessed the surrender and panicked. Why did Duchin claim that he could not identify the shooter and then state that it was Kid? Had Duchin been coached by the judge advocate, or was he just an unreliable witness? Certainly Chew's testimony made sense and was more reliable.

After calling Tony, a first sergeant of scouts, to testify the judge advocate asked if he knew the name of the defendant. Tony replied, "His Indian name is Hahouantell, white men call him Kid." After Tony heard several shots, he came out with his rifle and fired twice at the renegades. Asked if he knew who was doing the firing, he replied: "I was running from them. I don't know who did it." He said that he knew only one of them. "His name is Bachoandoth." He also saw John, another scout, fire at the renegades.[27]

The judge advocate summoned W. B. Horton, as interpreter, and then called Antonio Díaz to testify for the prosecution. Díaz declared that he was with Captain Pierce and Al Sieber when the scouts came in to surrender. Díaz asked Kid where he had been. Kid replied, "We have been off and have killed a man at the Aravaipa." The witness then said to him, "I am sorry." Kid replied, "It is no matter of yours nor of the [Indian] agent. It is our affair and no one else's." Díaz answered sarcastically, "That is all right, it does not matter to me whether you kill ten or a dozen Indians a day, and I suppose it does not matter to the Captain either."[28] Díaz remembered that he began to lecture Kid on responsibility and doing the right thing. This lecture on responsibility by Díaz suggests that he knew that Kid had violated the trust of the other four scouts when he decided to leave San Carlos to kill Rip and, apparently, had failed to consider the consequences of his action. Kid's obligations as a sergeant of scouts included being accountable for leading his scouts and looking out for them, and he also had Apache responsibilities for their welfare, as dictated by his SI band. Kid apparently did not consider the repercussions that his actions might entail by violating military rules.

Díaz asked Kid, "How is it that you have gone forty miles from here, killed a man in cold blood and returned here? It is not our custom to kill people thus." Kid replied, "Yes, but we did it. It is nobody's business." Díaz was suggesting that Kid had violated military rules by going off and killing another Apache. Díaz may have felt that since he was very familiar with Apache culture he had the right to dress Kid down for his behavior. Little is known about Díaz, but some think that as a Mexican youth he had been captured and raised by Apaches.[29] Because of his experiences he had gained a dislike for the Apaches at San Carlos, and apparently many of them distrusted him as well. It should be remembered that the Mexican government paid bounties for Apache scalps; consequently, Apaches hated Mexicans. After arriving at Sieber's tent, the witness said that he saw Kid immediately give up his gun. He claimed that when the captain said "calaboose," Bachoandoth, one of the scouts, stepped up to get his belt and then quickly grabbed one of the guns in front of him. At that time Kid was still standing there. Díaz claimed that when Bachoandoth stepped forward to get his belt he "suspected mischief." The witness stated that Bachoandoth said: "There is nothing for us to do but fight." Díaz, trying to get out of the way, fell down as he was backing up. Then Díaz "ran in the direction of the trader's store." Rowdy, another scout, fired a shot from near the scout's tent. Díaz conceded that he did not recognize the Indian who fired from the hill as they escaped. The witness acknowledged that he did not see anyone else grab a gun because his attention "was particularly directed to those Indians [on horseback] who were in front" of Sieber's tent. Asked by the judge advocate about the identity of these Indians, he replied, "I remember particularly Miguel, a Yaqui, and Gonshayee. He had no arms." He also testified that he saw Bachoandoth and Miguel fire their weapons "in the direction of the tent."[30] This testimony by the witness suggests that he had either forgotten the details of what had happened or he was twisting his facts for other reasons. For example, he claimed that apparently Bachoandoth tried to get his weapon before the shooting started. That makes no sense when compared with the testimony of Captain Pierce and other witnesses.

Baldwin began his cross-examination by asking how long Díaz had been an interpreter at San Carlos. The witness replied, "About four years and eight months." Counsel asked for the name of the man killed on the Aravaipa. Witness: "He was called 'Rip.'"[31] Asked whether Kid's being there was because of the killing of Rip, Díaz replied, "The Captain did not say anything to me about" Rip's death. Díaz admitted that he "was excited when the shooting began." Counsel: "If you fell back and did not devote much attention to . . . Captain Pierce and Sieber, and then ran around the tent and ran home like a deer, how can you swear on your oath that you saw Bachoandoth shoot at Captain Pierce, and Miguel fire a shot toward the tent?" He repeated his earlier testimony that Bachoandoth grabbed a rifle and both he and Miguel fired at the tent.[32] Díaz never mentioned what he had actually said to Kid about going to the calaboose. Díaz, of course, did not want to admit that he had warned them that they would be sent to Florida if they refused to obey Captain

Pierce. It is presumed that Baldwin should have known what Kid would say in his closing statement about Díaz's threat of being sent to Florida. This would have been the right time to argue that their actions were caused by panic and spontaneity rather than being planned. If it were the latter, why did they surrender their rifles? Sieber, of course, had argued that he thought the scouts had a prearranged signal, but Captain Pierce disagreed, concluding that they were indeed panicked by Díaz's statement. It certainly would have been useful for Baldwin to argue that Kid and his scouts did not actually mutiny but had been driven to escape by the shots fired by Miguel and SI band members and the chaos that followed.

The next day, defense counsel cross-examined Al Sieber in his quarters. Sieber testified that he had known Kid for about eight years and that he had "been a soldier four or five years out of the eight." Counsel asked whether Kid gained possession of any arms. Sieber: "No, sir." Baldwin asked if "the Indians on horse back looked hostile." Sieber: "Yes, my impression was that they looked hostile." He also admitted that he said nothing to Captain Pierce about his impressions. Baldwin: "Could not the cross look and gruff manner of the accused . . . have been the result of other causes than any hostile feeling in anticipation of an outbreak?" Sieber replied: "Yes they might have been caused by some other feelings." Counsel: "Do you understand the Apache language?" Sieber: "Not thoroughly." Sieber admitted that "there was no cry given by any of the scouts." Baldwin asked what happened to Kid after the shooting. Sieber testified that Kid began to run around the tent and was jumping in and out of shadows and bright sunlight. It is possible that Sieber had been blinded by the sun's rays, and this might explain why he testified that Kid had grabbed for his rifle. The evidence suggests panic, not the intent to mutiny. Asked whether Kid had any belts or weapons, Sieber replied, "He did not." When counsel asked about the character of the accused, Sieber replied, "His general character has always been good."[33]

*

Troopers' camp at San Carlos Agency, 1883. Courtesy Arizona State Library,
Archives and Public Records, History and Archives Division, Phoenix, #97-0512

Lieutenant Baldwin called Gonshayee as the first witness for the defense. The chief testified that he was with the Apaches who accompanied Kid when he surrendered to Captain Pierce. When asked whether the scouts had made an "arrangement that if Kid was sent to the guardhouse that it would be resisted," Gonshayee replied: "I don't know whether they made any arrangement about it before they came in or not." Questioned whether Kid had any arms when he fled, Gonshayee replied, "He had no arms, he had given them up before." During cross-examination the judge advocate asked, "When did you see Kid again after you saw him at the Indian hospital?" Gonshayee replied: "I saw him afterwards way up the Gila [River]." Questioned whether Kid had a horse, the witness testified that he was on foot. Asked where he went after the shooting in front of Al Sieber's tent, Gonshayee replied: "I went right between the school buildings in front of the officer's tent." Asked how he came to meet Kid on the Gila, Gonshayee responded: "Kid got up there on foot, of course he is better than a horse, can run better than a horse. We were looking for each other. We met coming from various directions."[34] This last testimony, showing Kid as a young Apache with great physical strength and stamina, may help explain why his scouts thought so much of him and would follow him anywhere. They respected his skills and, unfortunately, his judgment, thinking that he would know the right thing to do under such circumstances.

Gonshayee was a poor witness and failed to help defend Kid against the mutiny charges. Gonshayee may have been jealous and a divisive force within the SI band. In May 1888, Vacasheviejo, a member of the SI band, testified during Gonshayee's murder trial that he had bragged about killing William Diehl during the June 1887 raid. This later testimony suggests that this unsavory band chief might have been trying to impress his tribal members that he was a strong leader by killing a white man.[35] At any rate, Gonshayee's testimony proved to be rather negative and of little use in the defense of Kid. It is important to note that Baldwin confronted a difficult language barrier that put him at a great disadvantage.

Defense called Sayes, an SI band member, to testify. The judge advocate objected to the witness because he was one of the members involved in the mutiny. After discussion by both counsels, Sayes was permitted to testify. Asked where he was when Kid came in, Sayes replied, "I was on horseback near Sieber's tent that evening." Baldwin asked whether the scouts had an understanding that if they "were sent to the guardhouse that they would resist?" After objection from the judge advocate, he was allowed to answer the question. Sayes: "No sir." Baldwin asked whether there was any understanding that they would resist. The judge advocate objected that counsel was leading the witness. Counsel explained to the court that it was difficult to get the witness to understand and therefore he needed to ask the question. Because of the witness's inability to understand English, Baldwin insisted that "this question should be allowed." The objection by the judge advocate was not sustained by the court panel. Sayes answered: "No sir. Those fellows that were with the scouts came down for the scouts' horses." In other words there was no agreement among Gonshayee's band to take action. Counsel asked what the scouts who were coming in intended to do. Sayes explained that Kid told the scouts, "We will obey orders whatever Sieber says." In cross-examination the judge advocate asked whether Kid was on a horse, and Sayes answered no. Tyson asked whether he was related to Kid, and Sayes stated: "I am not any relation to him."[36]

Lieutenant Baldwin began the next stage of his defense by introducing four discharge papers from the U.S. Army to document the character of First Sergeant Kid. These documents revealed that Kid's services as a scout had been excellent for the periods 1882, 1883, and 1884. After a brief discussion the judge advocate accepted the documents as evidence of Kid's service as a scout.[37] Baldwin introduced these documents to show that Kid was a soldier for only brief periods during each of these four enlistments.

Baldwin had no more witnesses, but the defendant wanted to make a statement on his own behalf. The judge advocate agreed to allow him to speak. Kid stated: "I left here without permission from Sieber or the Captain. I went up to camp and I drank a whole lot of tiswin and . . . we went down to kill 'Rip' on the Aravaipa. Rip is the man who put up a job to kill my grandfather and Rip said, 'I shall kill you. I have killed several Indians but I never have been tried.' As soon as I got up to Rip's camp I saw Rip and shot him. After that I came back, I had been absent five days." In this statement Kid was noting that Rip had been neither punished by Apache law nor indicted nor tried by the Gila County civil authorities. Kid stated that he thought about coming back to San Carlos, and finally, after sending Gonshayee to negotiate with Captain Pierce and Sieber, he agreed to come in and submit to any punishment by Sieber and Pierce. "I told all the Scouts they must give up their arms and to obey orders."[38]

Kid remembered that when Captain Pierce arrived at Sieber's tent he ordered Kid and his scouts to give up their guns and belts. Kid stated: "I laid my gun on the ground and the belt on the chair." Sieber spoke up and said go to the calaboose, meaning they should go to the guardhouse. Kid testified that Antonio Díaz, the interpreter, spoke to them in Apache, saying, "'All the Indians that don't obey the orders, will be sent to Florida.' At the same time all the Indians [Gonshayee and his SI band members] outside made a noise and were much excited about what Antonio had spoke. I thought those outside thought then that we Scouts would be sent down to Florida. At the same time I heard a shot. I was . . . facing Sieber, a chair was standing between him and me. . . . Sieber grabbed the guns and at the same time I skipped out and did not pay any attention to getting a gun." Kid remembered that he heard several rapid shots at about the same time. Kid said "[I] went in front of Indian Hospital and behind officers tents, I was without arms. I looked back and saw Tony shoot at me twice the bullets striking close to me on the ground. I was on foot and went down towards the river." Kid stated that when he ran by the mill, heading toward the Gila River, Indian scouts shot at him. Kid testified that he met up with the other scouts and SI band members on a hill overlooking the Gila River.[39]

Kid stated: "After that I went away and I got back here after being absent twenty-five days. When I was out in the mountains General Miles sent word to me that I must come back that it would be better for me and all my people." Kid continued, "I had been obeying orders, but God sent bad spirits in my heart. I think you all know all the people can't get along very well in the world. There are some good people and some bad people amongst them all." By suggesting "bad spirits" he may have been having second thoughts about killing Rip or for letting his scouts get involved, which put them in jeopardy. Kid declared: "If I had made any arrangement before I came in, I would not have given up my arms at Mr. Sieber's tent." Finally, Kid explained, "I am not afraid to tell all these things because I have not done very much harm. I killed only one man whose name is 'Rip' because he killed my grandfather. I am not educated like you and therefore can't say very much."[40] This testimony clearly indicates that Kid, while serving as a scout, knew that he had to obey the orders of Captain Pierce and Sieber. He believed that killing Rip was an SI band responsibility, but he admitted it was wrong to leave the reservation to enforce traditional tribal law. Kid suggested that if he had more education he would have been able to persuade the officers on the court-martial panel to understand the truth as he saw it from an Apache perspective. Kid's statement was consistent with virtually all of the testimony taken previously and never contradicted. He was being frank and up front about what had happened, demonstrating his apparent belief in the process even if he did not understand it. Kid's testimony reveals that he trusted General Miles enough to put himself at the mercy of military justice. He believed that Miles would treat him fairly. Tyson chose not to cross-examine Kid.

It is interesting to note that Kid did not mention the earlier testimony by Antonio Díaz, who claimed that the defendant had failed to look after the welfare of his scouts, especially those who were married and had family responsibilities. Díaz, with more than four years of interpreting service for the U.S. Army, had spent years dealing with the Apaches; consequently, he knew that band chiefs and subchiefs had to be responsible for the safety of their followers. Kid, of course, fit into this category. As first sergeant of Apache scouts he was duty bound to look out for their welfare. Kid, no doubt, was unhappy with Díaz's condescending statement about his neglect of tribal obligations. Kid realized that his actions had put his scouts and their families in danger. He could have instructed them to remain at San Carlos while he traveled south to take retribution against Rip. That, however, would have gone against Apache social traditions. After all, they were also SI band members who must have hated Rip for killing their chief. All of these issues weighed heavily on Kid's mind; he realized that he had let his scouts down.

We have only seven hundred words spoken by Kid when he addressed the court-martial panel on his own behalf. He related only how and why he got into trouble and tried to explain his actions and the events that took place. Of the forty-one lines of text, twenty-eight deal with Kid's problems with the U.S. Army and the other thirteen address Rip, his grandfather Togodechuz, and spiritual issues. Kid's words reveal that he had returned to his Apache mode of thinking. These are not the words he might have used as an army scout. In his discussion of the mutiny he provides a straightforward account that fits the evidence presented in his court-martial. He admitted that he had left his duty station without permission and had violated military rules. He also stated that although he had killed one man, he had "not done very much harm." In the second section, one immediately notices that some of his words suggest the metaphysical; the main focus is on his grandfather and the spiritual realm. Further, he refers to good and bad people, God and his grandfather, and Rip. Among the Apaches the maternal grandfather is always the mentor and spiritual leader for a young boy. Consequently, Kid could think of nothing else; he loved his grandfather, and Rip had him killed. Kid seemed obsessed with killing Rip; in his statement he mentions Rip seven times and uses the word *kill* six. He had six months to commiserate and brood about his grandfather's death, which explains why it became the undivided focus of his thinking and decisive actions. It had harmed him deeply, it had to be answered, he had to kill Rip, it was his duty as an SI band Apache, and it was the right, the Apache, thing to do. Kid had maintained a close bond with his grandfather, who had confided ceremonial knowledge about the spiritual world.[41] We don't know exactly what Kid was thinking about his grandfather; however, his statement suggests that he had been deeply traumatized by the killing of Togodechuz. Gonshayee probably had urged Kid to kill Rip, and the young scout responded with action.

Since Kid felt that it was his obligation under Apache law to kill Rip, one wonders why he did not say so in his statement? Or maybe he actually did. The statement "I killed only one man" in Apache would be a rather complicated passage that could have been misconstrued.[42] It is possible that he said that it was his tribal duty to kill Rip, and the interpreters missed it or thought that it was unimportant. Kid also mentioned that he "went up to the foot of the mountain" while he thought about what he should do. This passage deals with the metaphysical world. Since it was common among the Apaches to travel to a sacred site such as a mountain or somewhere nearby to meditate and resolve their problems, this may be what Kid is referring to. Further, he stated that he "had been obeying orders, but God sent bad spirits in my heart," and then mentioned that there were "some good people and some bad people" in the world. These passages not only indicate a strong spiritual tone but also suggest that their importance and meaning bring into question the veracity of the translation of his statement by Shago and Robert McIntosh.

Kid's words offer some intriguing questions about just how accurately they were translated by the two interpreters. First, the translation seems too smooth and polished for testimony given in Apache then converted to Spanish and finally to English. Could the translation have been that perfect? Second, just how accomplished were McIntosh and Shago, who interpreted at Kid's court-martial? Did they translate from Apache to Spanish first, or straight to English? There is no mention of exactly how it was accomplished in the court-martial transcript. For example, take the words father and grandfather. The transcript reads that it was Kid's grandfather who had been killed, and that was accepted by the court-martial panel, General Miles, and Lieber. No one questioned its veracity. Most of the secondary literature on Kid, however, claims that it was his father who had been killed by Rip's band. In Western Apache *father* would be *shitaa* and *grandfather, shidaalé*.[43] Could those two words have been misinterpreted? It might have been possible and may help to explain the existence of two different versions of who had been killed, Kid's father or grandfather. Also open to question is whether Kid and the interpreters spoke the same dialect. There are five groups of Western Apaches broken down into at least twenty bands with slightly differing dialects. Perhaps Shago spoke in a Tonto or Cibecue dialect, while Kid was speaking Aravaipa or San Carlos, which might have had slightly different sounds when being pronounced. It is possible that the interpreters made mistakes on the dialect differences. It opens up the possibility that there could have been some mistranslation in Kid's statement and those of the other Apache witnesses as well. Getting this statement translated correctly is critical in trying to understand exactly what

Kid had felt and what he really believed. We will never know the answer to this intriguing question.

Defense counsel began his summation by asserting that the officers were trying Kid not only as a soldier of the U.S. Army but also as an Indian. Baldwin was about to focus on the dichotomy of Kid's living in two worlds without knowing which rules to accept, military or Apache. Baldwin stated, "This brings before us two facts. One, the Indian civilization of the nineteenth century, the other the alleged crime of Mutiny." Defense counsel realized that trying an Indian for mutiny, a charge that Kid most likely did not fully understand, revealed a prejudice against his client. Baldwin challenged the judge advocate to establish his theory that Kid and his scouts had prearranged to mutiny when they arrived to surrender. Baldwin argued that the evidence presented did not withstand the test of cross-examination. Speaking of testimony by the prosecution's witnesses, defense counsel continued, "Did they hear him say anything that indicated insubordinate intentions. I answer for him and them—No."

Turning to a discussion of Sieber's claim that Kid made a look that suggested a preconceived plan to mutiny, counsel stated sarcastically: "If I may quote a line of poetry. 'My chosen braves rush for your guns.' "[44] Baldwin may have decided to discredit Sieber's testimony because he was a civilian, while Captain Pierce, who had extensive service and had dealt with Indians for more than a decade, would be more believable. It seemed logical that the panel would prefer to believe a fellow officer instead of a civilian scout. Counsel reiterated that none of the witnesses at Sieber's tent had implicated the defendant in a wrongful act. He also explained that when Kid returned to see Sieber he was contrite about his "previous errors," and he had submitted to the authority of the chief of scouts. The testimony of Sieber and Pierce conflicts, Sieber claiming that Kid tried to get his gun, while Pierce testified otherwise. The evidence reveals that Kid fled without either a weapon or a horse. Baldwin argued that the defendant, a scout with six years' experience, had submitted and stood "with head bent and silent of tongue perchance trying to hide the shame of his disgrace, by being degraded full in the sight of his people."[45] This is an important point. Kid was surrendering not only to the military but also in front of Gonshayee, SI band chief, and other members of his clan. Since he had important status within his band as well as influence and power over his scouts, it must have been very humiliating.

Turning to a discussion of what actually took place in front of Al Sieber's tent, counsel again became sarcastic, claiming that Antonio Díaz, the "prophet" and "the staunch friend of the prosecution," testified that he saw one of the scouts grab a gun, "fire a shot in the direction of Captain Pierce and Sieber, and cry out 'there is nothing for us to do but fight.' " Despite what Díaz claimed he heard, neither Pierce nor Sieber heard this alleged declaration or witnessed Kid or any other scout grab and fire a weapon. As both witnesses had been standing next to the weapons and ammunition belts, they could not have missed these actions. Equally important, all of the gunfire came from the SI band members on horseback who had been watching the surrender. Baldwin explained that although some of the prosecution witnesses who worked for the government suggested, in hindsight, that they had harbored "suspicions of trouble" and claimed that they "saw a supposed warlike array," none of them "uttered a note of warning" to Captain Pierce. Counsel argued that Captain Pierce had exhibited no fear or concern when the scouts came up to Sieber's tent. Baldwin: "I ask, would those scouts have surrendered their arms, if any prearrangement had been entered into, any signal agreed upon?" Instead of resisting, they had vanished. Baldwin argued: "True to the traditions of his race, at the sound of turbulent strife he fled unarmed, why, because the history of his people has taught him to scan with suspicious eye the figure of justice when a white man and an Indian is concerned." Baldwin explained that Kid was fortunate to be brought before this court that would refuse to judge him in the "atmosphere of prejudice" that surrounds the Apaches in Arizona Territory. He believed that the court would realize that Kid, "a stranger to our language, unconscious of our laws, customs, and habits," came from a very different world, and, based upon the evidence, they would try him fairly.[46] Despite Baldwin's eloquence he was dealing with a group of soldiers who held a low opinion of Apaches, thought alike, and shared a belief in military solidarity—a court-martial panel that had already exhibited bias against Kid.

Baldwin easily dismantled the testimony of Duchin, the blacksmith, demonstrating that according to the rules of criminal evidence his testimony revealed prejudice and was "valueless in comparison with that of unbiased witnesses." Duchin had testified that he had seen the accused fire a "shot from a point between an outhouse and the dormitory" on a line of fire that "was in sight of many who witnessed" the events in front of Sieber's tent. Baldwin stated that no other eyewitnesses had corroborated the testimony of Duchin.

In his final summation of the evidence against Kid, Baldwin argued, "You may not believe the evidence of the Indians who gave testimony if you rely upon the opinions of the Judge Advocate, but . . . they have been un-impeached, on the contrary they have been corroborated."[47] Counsel cautioned the court that Indian testimony, confirmed by Sieber and Captain Pierce, showed that the accused was unarmed. Further, when witnesses saw Kid later on the Gila River he was still unarmed and on foot. Baldwin contended that in order to convict the defendant for the crime of mutiny, the prosecution had to prove that there was intent. Counsel argued that the evidence showed that Kid was "only present at the outbreak, he aided not, he assisted not, he countenanced not, he abetted not, but quick to fear the white man . . . he fled unarmed."[48] In another venue or time this argument should have led to acquittal on the charge of mutiny, but this was San Carlos, and these were army officers with a decided point of view on the charge.

Baldwin asked the panel: "Is there any evidence that this defendant resisted arrest, seized his arms or fired upon his Commanding Officer? If there is no evidence against him is he not innocent?" Counsel argued that although Kid was a scout, "his childlike faith in the superior wisdom of those controlling his destinies caused him to submit to the deprivations of many of his rights as a soldier." Baldwin was talking about Kid not only as a soldier with military rights and duties but also as an Indian, reacting as an Apache, "childlike." On the one hand Baldwin was trying to protect Kid's rights as a soldier by insisting that he was a soldier. On the other hand Baldwin was also trying to obtain mitigation on the grounds that Kid was an Indian. His argument fell on deaf ears with the panel; however, this legal discussion struck a cord with General Miles. Returning to his argument, Baldwin cautioned the court members that they were "sitting in judgment upon the Indian civilization of this country. . . . If this defendant has done wrong he awaits your verdict. He came here voluntarily, he cannot see . . . where he has erred beyond an absence. He fears no punishment that right and justice will decree." Finally, in his eloquent closing statement Baldwin tried to appeal to the mercy of the court: "From the silent gorges and rocky fastnesses of the serried mountains that dot the face of this desolate country, at the bidding of General Miles the defendant came back and surrendered."[49] Counsel argued that based upon the evidence the court should find the accused not guilty on both charges. Tyson chose not to rebut the defense's summation. No doubt, with the solidarity of the panel he felt confident that he would win his case.

Baldwin stood bravely against the panel even though he was swimming upstream. He seemed to have a strategy that focused on bringing these issues to the attention of General Miles and the judge advocate general. Baldwin made sure that Kid received a full trial with all protections accorded and argued in court. That in itself was a remarkable achievement. Counsel was not going through the motions like the defender of the Cibecue mutiny defendants; he provided a strong, well-reasoned defense. Early in the trial Baldwin briefly explained the dichotomy of "Indian civilization" and military culture.

Baldwin understood that Kid was torn between his cultural responsibilities as an Apache and his duties as a soldier. Baldwin's argument shows that he understood the significance of this dangerous middle ground. In his summation Baldwin used the word *Indian* twenty-two times. Baldwin explained "that in trying this defendant as a soldier of the United States Army we are trying him also as an Indian."[50] This was the point in the summation where Baldwin made a strong argument that Kid, or any other Apache, did not understand what mutiny really meant or how it could be accomplished. Baldwin emphasized that what happened in front of Sieber's tent suggested spontaneity and panic, not a planned mutiny. Since the defendants were Apache scouts when Díaz made the threatening statement about the scouts' being exiled to Florida, it frightened the SI band members who were watching their surrender. As noted earlier in 1886, despite their devoted service to the U.S. Army, the Chiricahua scouts who had hunted down Geronimo were all sent to Florida. In other words, the threat, coming so soon after the banishment of a large number of loyal scouts, seemed real. It is possible that Baldwin did not argue more about Díaz's statement because that might bring out the Cibecue mutiny, which must have been on the minds of the panel.

Baldwin made two critical points. In terms of legal rights Kid was a soldier like them; nevertheless, he remained an Apache who had observed the duplicity of white men in Arizona Territory. Baldwin was trying to show his fellow officers that Kid was conflicted by the complex world around him; he thought like an Apache while serving as an enlisted member of the army. It seems clear that these officers had little understanding of Kid's world. They were only intent on convicting the Apache scouts to send a strong message to the others: if you mutiny you will pay a heavy price, as did the three scouts at Cibecue in 1881. Defense counsel may have already realized that the court-martial panel was going to be harsh in its decision and penalty; therefore, since all of this testimony and his summation would become part of the official transcript, Baldwin may have been arguing to influence General Miles and the judge advocate general. They would review the final decision of the court. Baldwin was arguing for the benefit of the reviewers, who would immediately recognize that the trial was unfair. It proved to be an effective strategy. From the very beginning Baldwin must have known that it would have been almost impossible to convince a panel of officers who had little respect for Indian culture, least of all Apaches. Consequently, he played his trump card by speaking not to the court-martial panel but to General Miles and the judge advocate general. Baldwin had provided a strong, sound defense for Kid.

After the courtroom was cleared, the court-martial panel began its deliberations and in a brief period of time reconvened the proceedings and announced its verdict. The panel concluded that, after "having maturely considered the evidence adduced," it found the accused First Sergeant Kid guilty on both charges of desertion and mutiny. By a two-thirds majority they sentenced Kid to death. At least six of the eight court members voted for the death penalty as required by military law.[51] This verdict attests to the solidarity of the officers on the panel, who probably viewed the general court-martial of Kid as fair under military law; after all, they were only punishing a soldier who had violated military rules, putting the lives of others in jeopardy. It probably never occurred to the officers that they were making a "cultural" not "legal" judgment; they believed that their actions were standard operating procedure. They probably viewed Kid as a barbaric Apache, uncouth and unable to speak good English. But at the same time they understood that he was still an enlisted soldier and, as far as they were concerned, he should have known and obeyed military rules. The members of the panel had been well-versed in military law at either the Military Academy or by self-study. Accordingly, they asserted that they could try the defendant fairly and administer justice, and it seems clear that they believed that they had served justice with their verdict. Nevertheless, it also seems obvious that the final verdict reached by the officers does not agree with the evidence. The facts of the case reveal that Kid had not mutinied, that many of the officers were biased against Apaches, and that their treatment of Kid, a cultural judgment by the military, was unfair.

In analyzing the harsh verdict of the court-martial panel it must be understood that many of them were experienced army officers who believed in dealing harshly with soldiers accused of desertion and mutiny. During the late nineteenth century many of the enlisted men recruited into the U.S. Army were recent German and Irish immigrants, and they, along with the Apache scouts, were held in low regard by the officers, who believed that many were untrustworthy. Since they were seen as "foreigners" with weak language skills and unaccustomed to American cultural values, army officers shared no common bond with them, especially the Apache scouts. To make matters worse, during this period enlisted men lived under substandard conditions on military posts throughout the American West. They received poor-quality food cooked badly, were required to perform hours of "fatigue" or manual labor, drank and gambled to excess, and were subjected to harsh punishment by their officers for minor infractions of military regulations. These conditions contributed to high desertion rates throughout the late nineteenth century, and officers who sat in judgment on courts-martial panels convicted them.[52]

These factors, of course, help to explain the decision of the court-martial panel. Kid fell into this category of unreliable men that officers believed had to be controlled at all costs. His being an Apache, considered by many whites to be a "savage," made it even easier for the officers to reach their decision. Kid's misfortune proved to be the absence of any officers on the panel, such as Lieutenants Britton Davis or Charles B. Gatewood, who understood the Apaches and sympathized with their plight at the hands of white authorities. Both of those officers served at San Carlos and Fort Apache and later wrote books that dealt with the unfair treatment of the Apaches.[53] Such voices of moderation did not exist on this or probably any other court-martial panel trying Apache scouts for violations of military law.

The guilty verdict on the lesser charge of desertion against Kid certainly does not fit the facts presented during the court-martial. To substantiate a charge of desertion it was necessary to establish that the person was absent without authority and that he had no intention of returning. Mitigating circumstances in a soldier's alleged guilt of being absent without leave might include that he was under the influence of liquor and that he returned voluntarily after a brief absence.[54] Both of these conditions applied to Kid and his four scouts. They were indeed under the influence of tiswin, and they did return voluntarily to San Carlos to surrender. Even after they went on their raid, Kid and his scouts agreed to return and submit to any punishment ordered by General Miles. Other legitimate mitigating factors might be that the accused was young and inexperienced, that his commanding officer had never explained the Articles of War to him, and that he "did not comprehend the gravity of the offence." After several years of service as a scout Kid obviously was neither young nor inexperienced. There is little doubt, however, that he was unable to fully understand the Articles of War. Captain Pierce admitted that no one had instructed Kid on the requirements of the articles.

The final punishment of the deserter is within the discretion of the court to decide, but the death penalty is seldom administered except during times of war. Graduates of the U.S. Military Academy received training in military law that included discussions on the Articles of War. Panel members understood that they were required to explain them to their enlisted men.[55] The guilty verdict on the more serious charge of mutiny also defies logic. There is little doubt that Díaz's threatening comment about being exiled to Florida was what precipitated the "mutiny." Even Captain Pierce concluded that there was no threat prior to Díaz's comment. It seems clear that the scouts' actions were caused by panic, not open rebellion. It would be hard to conclude that it was mutiny.

There is, however, another possibility that needs to be explored. Historian Dan Thrapp suggested "that it was a drumhead court" that was "merely a formality" before punishment.[56] Such military legal actions were really summary justice and were originally used by the British Navy to discipline sailors accused of various infractions, including mutiny. The holding of these tribunals on board ship was accompanied by drumming to assure that every sailor came to watch and understood the consequences of the offense committed. Winthrop explained that a "Drum Head Court was considered to be permissible only in an emergency, as during war or the occasion of a mutiny." He also noted that "no such court has ever been sanctioned in our law or practice."[57] There is, however, at least one case documented during the Civil War, when General James A. Garfield ordered a drumhead court that tried and executed two Confederate spies caught while wearing U.S. Army uniforms in June 1863.[58] Drumhead courts were also practiced during World War II, and this type of summary legal action is still controversial. For example, some legal authorities believe that the military tribunals ordered to try alleged "enemy combatants" detained at Guantanamo Bay fit within this category. In Kid's case, the evidence strongly suggests that his court-martial shared some similarities with a drumhead court and that the court panel was just going through the motions.

But was it a drumhead court? Thrapp may be wrong. On the one hand, the Articles of War mandated a short time frame of eight days to order a court-martial. This made a fair trial nearly impossible under the conditions that existed on the frontier, where it was difficult to find enough officers for court duty. The hierarchical, authoritarian nature of the military and the fact that an Indian was on trial made the defense lawyer's job almost impossible. No doubt General Miles realized that these officers would convict Kid and order the death penalty. Although General Miles had to act within eight days, he found a good, sympathetic lawyer. Considering the primitive conditions that existed on the frontier, that in itself seems like a virtual miracle. Further, Miles was able to guarantee a quorum by calling up reserve panelists. Therefore, under these unreasonable conditions virtually every court-martial on the frontier might be described as a drumhead court. On the other hand, despite the inevitable time constraints and a court-martial panel that some might call hostile, Baldwin gave a thorough and well-calculated defense. He cross-examined the prosecution's witnesses, called witnesses for the defense, and allowed Kid to testify. In other words, military law did include due process under the Articles of War. Part of this process included the challenge by defense counsel, mitigating powers of the commanding officer, and the final review by the Judge Advocate General's Department. This due process required by the Articles of War would suggest that it was not a drumhead court. Due process will be discussed in more detail later.

Finally, one wonders whether Kid really understood his responsibilities as a sergeant of scouts. His testimony and that of Díaz, the interpreter, reveal that Kid knew that he had violated military rules and would be punished upon his return to San Carlos. Kid testified that General Miles assured him that he must return; it would be best for him, his scouts, and his SI band members. He may have felt guilty about getting his scouts involved in the blood feud killing of Rip; it put them in jeopardy with the army and endangered these men, who had responsibilities to their own families. By pleading ignorance of military rules Kid may have been playing dumb during his court-martial. No doubt he lacked formal education in English, but it is hard to believe that a first sergeant of scouts, with approximately five years of intermittent service, would not understand that if he went absent without leave he would be punished. In case one might think that Kid was just a pawn of the whites and only being acted upon by Captain Pierce and Al Sieber, it seems clear that Kid made choices—bad ones at that, but they were his to make and he paid the price for his lack of good judgment. There is little doubt that Kid believed his responsibility to tribal law took precedence over military

obligation: he had to kill Rip in retaliation for the death of his grandfather. He knew that he was taking a risk by leaving his duty post at San
Carlos; that is why he waited until Pierce and Sieber traveled to Fort
Apache. Kid knew he would be punished; that is the reason he sent
Gonshayee, acting as a mediator, to see Captain Pierce about coming in
to surrender. Kid's behavior suggests that he was acting like a prisoner of
war rather than a deserter. Unfortunately, by leaving his post Kid set off a
chain of events that included the deaths of two white citizens and ended
in the prosecution of five of his band members for murder. Askisaylala
and Nahconquisay, two of his scouts, and Gonshayee paid with their lives
for the crimes they had committed during the raid. Kid's reckless behavior had triggered a human disaster for him and his SI band.

THE APPEALS

While the prisoners are enlisted scouts, the evidence shows them to be ignorant, unlettered Indians, requiring even the rendering of the language of the Court through two languages or mediums to convey to them an idea of what was said and done before the court in their cases. . . . [They are] uninstructed in the code of crimes and punishments prescribed by the Articles of War; unfamiliar with the discipline of the service and uninformed as to the responsibilities of a soldier.

GENERAL NELSON A. MILES, "Orders to Major Anson Mills, Presiding Officer, Regarding Changes in Court-Martial of First Sergeant Kid," 1887

·   ·   ·

No findings or sentence recommended by a court-martial panel could be enforced without the approval of the commanding officer who had ordered the court-martial and by the Judge Advocate General's Department. The commanding officer who authorized the general court-martial had the power to pardon or mitigate or reduce any punishment recommended by the panel.[1] Pardon or mitigation was fairly common for a defendant who was "a recruit or young and inexperienced, or a foreigner with an imperfect understanding of English." After the proceedings were finally approved by the commanding officer, the judge advocate would immediately forward the full proceedings directly to the Judge Advocate General's Department in Washington, D.C., for further legal review.[2]

With the ratification of the U.S. Constitution, Congress received powers to regulate the military and on July 16, 1794, appointed

Campbell Smith as the first judge advocate general of the newly organized U.S. Army. During the next half-century Congress periodically
revised the Articles of War and appointed additional judge advocates for
each military division. On June 20, 1864, during the Civil War, the
Bureau of Military Justice became part of the War Department and
served as the archival repository of all courts-martial records from the
various military districts.[3] The duties of the judge advocate general included receiving, revising, and recording all military legal transcripts
while acting as the legal adviser to the secretary of war and the President
on all issues arising from courts-martial conducted throughout the U.S.
Army. The judge advocate general examined and wrote legal opinions on
those cases that merited his attention. This office could be considered an
appellate tribunal especially when examining the more serious cases that
included the death penalty.[4] The judge advocate general's advice would
certainly be important in cases sent to the President for a final decision.
During the nineteenth century the judge advocate general's staff in the
Bureau of Military Justice received, recorded, reviewed and filed thousands of court-martial transcripts and required a sizable number of military lawyers to accomplish this task.

     After the Civil War Congress began to look for ways to cut the mil-
itary budget and in 1874 decided to reduce the judge advocate general's
budget significantly. This legislation abolished the office of assistant
judge advocate general and reduced the legal staff from eight to four
members. Because of the large numbers of court-martial records
received and reviewed, this would have created a serious burden for the
judge advocate general's staff. For example, from September 1, 1862,
through March 1, 1876, the department recorded 224,313 cases and
added them to more than 69,000 transcripts already on file. During
that same period the judge advocate general and his staff had written
34,923 legal opinions and reports, about 2,910 per year. With such a
heavy case load any personnel reductions would seriously harm the
performance of the U.S. Army's legal office. Judge Advocate General
W. McKee Dunn and his Bureau of Military Justice of course had sup-

porters who began to complain to Congress. In a report published in 1878, General Winfield S. Hancock explained that the "duties of Judge Advocates are inseparable from the military system," and therefore, they were essential for handling the legal needs of the U.S. Army. He suggested that judge advocates with a "thorough knowledge of military law . . . [are] particularly necessary in new armies" to assure that discipline and order are maintained. General Alfred H. Terry complained that "the Courts-Martial are composed of officers who, as a rule, are not versed in the law, who have no legal training." Terry lamented that, even more serious, "a person accused of a military offense is entitled to all the safeguards which those rules" afford him, and without a full staff at the Bureau of Military Justice any cases that revealed errors might not be fairly reviewed. Finally, General Stephen Vincent Benet believed that the legal opinions written by the "Bureau of Military Justice have contributed largely in establishing uniformity of practice and decision in the administration of justice by military courts."[5] Benet was concerned that a failure to assure proper legal review might cause serious damage to the U.S. Army. In 1878, with such strong pressure applied by ten U.S. Army generals, Congress relented and restored the staff to its original eight members.

In 1881 Colonel Winthrop, the leading reformer, who had been attached to the Bureau of Military Justice for over a decade, received a temporary appointment as acting judge advocate general; however, sixteen days later Major David G. Swaim, five years Winthrop's junior in service and with less legal experience, received an appointment to succeed Dunn as the judge advocate general. Since President Rutherford Hayes appointed the judge advocate general, it is possible that he was showing preference to a fellow Ohioan. Although Swaim had gained experience as a judge advocate, he had not practiced such duties during the Civil War. Winthrop, although better qualified, was reassigned to the Division of the Pacific, where he served for five years before returning to teach military law at the U.S. Military Academy in 1886. Two years earlier, Congress had passed legislation that finally combined the Bureau of

Military Justice and judge advocate general's staff into the Judge
Advocate General's Department.[6]

In a bizarre twist of fate, in 1884 Swaim was court-martialed, prosecuted by Major Asa Bird Gardiner, one of his own aides, and found
guilty of "improprieties in his conduct of a business transaction." This
was a remarkable court-martial, with such well-known generals as Alfred
H. Terry, Nelson A. Miles, and John B. Schofield serving on the panel.
Major Gardiner, the judge advocate, had a reputation for being one of
the best lawyers in the Judge Advocate General's Department. After
almost two months the court-martial panel found Swaim guilty. The
original sentence called for a three-year suspension from rank and duty.
President Chester A. Arthur, however, was unsatisfied and sent the transcript back to the court for revision. On February 16, 1885, the court
changed its sentence to suspension from rank and duty for twelve years,
and Swaim was ordered to forfeit half of his pay. Consequently, Swaim's
tenure as the top legal officer in the U.S. Army proved to be rather
unusual. Although suspended, he was nominally the judge advocate
general. Colonel G. Norman Lieber received an appointment to serve as
acting judge advocate general with lower pay and rank. Lieber held this
position and title from July 1884 until January 1895. Swaim, who sought
vindication, did not have his sentence remitted until December 1894.
He retired two weeks later.[7] Upon Swaim's retirement Colonel Lieber
finally was promoted to general and confirmed as the judge advocate
general, and he continued to serve in that position until his retirement
in May 1901.

Lieber, with impeccable legal credentials, was well qualified to be the
judge advocate general. He held degrees from the University of South
Carolina and Harvard Law School and had been admitted to the New
York bar in 1859. While serving in the military during the Civil War he
had garnered citations for gallantry in the battle of Gaines' Mill in 1862
and again in the Red River campaign in 1864. In 1867 he received an
appointment to major and was transferred to the Bureau of Military
Justice in Washington. From 1878 to 1882 he taught law at the U.S.

Military Academy, and in 1884 he received a promotion to colonel and became the acting judge advocate general. It is possible that Lieber taught military law to some of the officers involved in Kid's court-martial, such as panel members Lieutenants Elliot and Hughes, defense counsel Lieutenant Baldwin, and Judge Advocate Lieutenant Tyson, all of whom attended West Point during that period.[8] This might help to explain Baldwin's legal expertise, displayed ably in Kid's court-martial. Lieber is best known for his *Lieber on Army Regulations* and *The Use of the Army in Aid of the Civil Power*, both published in 1898.[9] It is also important to remember that Lieber opposed Winthrop on many legal issues and shared some of Sherman's legal philosophy that the general in the field must be in complete command in administering any general courts-martial.

Although the President was considered to be the final reviewing authority, the secretary of war acted as the final judge in Kid's case. Any decision made by the secretary of war was assumed to be the act of the President. During the appeals process the Judge Advocate General's Department assisted and advised the secretary of war in making his final decision on whether to modify the sentences of the five scouts or to confirm their punishment. In effect the judge advocate general's staff served as the "court of appeals" for all general court-martial cases. In essence, they were the final court, with the power to confirm or overturn the convictions and sentences of any court-martial case presented to them. After making his decision, the judge advocate general was required to forward his opinions and recommendations to the secretary of war, who then made the final decision—in this case, whether to remit the sentence that had been imposed or to enforce the punishment ordered by a court-martial.[10] Many of the legal staff at the Judge Advocate General's Department were not only trained in military and civil law but also highly experienced and had taught military law at the U.S. Military Academy. However, before the judge advocate general could take action on any court-martial, it was the duty of the commanding officer to initiate and complete a review of Kid's case either to approve or to disapprove of the

General Nelson A. Miles,
1880s. Courtesy Arizona
State Library, Archives and
Public Records, History and
Archives Division, Phoenix,
#97-7359

court panel's findings and sentence and then to forward the full transcript to the Judge Advocate General's Department.

General Nelson A. Miles brought a distinguished career in the U.S. Army
to Arizona Territory in 1886. He had been cited for gallantry during the
Civil War at the battles of the Wilderness, Spotsylvania Court House, and
Ream's Station and had received the Congressional Medal of Honor at the
Battle of Chancellorsville when he was severely wounded. In 1880 Miles
was promoted to brigadier general. Some of his fellow officers, such as
General George Crook, however, viewed him as "pompous, vain, grasping,
and morally dishonest in his dealings with the Indians," especially the
Apaches.[11] Miles no doubt shared the typical bias and prejudices of many
other white army officers under his command. As noted earlier, he had a

rather low opinion of Apaches, and in his reports and memoirs he referred to them as "savages" and "degraded and barbarous Indians."[12] Nevertheless, as will be demonstrated during his review of the court-martial findings, it seems clear that Miles really understood Kid's predicament and apparently felt sympathy for him. Miles had military law experience, which included serving on several high-profile court-martial panels, including the one held for U.S. Military Academy cadet Joseph C. Whittaker, a black man found guilty of "self-mutilation," though he testified that he had been attacked by other cadets. General Miles and four other officers urged clemency, and later President Chester A. Arthur threw out all of the charges on the grounds that the "court-martial was illegal."[13]

After receiving the transcript of Kid's court-martial, General Miles began his review of the panel's findings and sentence. On July 29, 1887, Miles returned the documents with instructions for the panel to reconvene and reexamine their verdict and sentence. After reconsidering the case, they revoked the first sentence and on August 6, 1887, submitted a second version recommending that the defendant "be confined at hard labor . . . for the period of his natural life." On December 27, 1887, still not satisfied, General Miles used his powers of mitigation to reduce the punishment to ten years to be served at Fort Leavenworth, Kansas; the sentence was later changed to confinement on Alcatraz Island.[14] It is possible that Miles used his mitigation powers to keep peace with the Apache scouts and the other Apaches at San Carlos. Miles had to provide some punishment to assuage the feelings of his officers on the court-martial panel, but after looking at their final sentence he must have seen the unfairness and acted accordingly.

On July 29, 1887, Lieutenant Charles B. Gatewood, aide-de-camp to General Miles, sent a message to Major Anson Mills with further instructions for the court-martial panel. Gatewood informed Mills that General Miles ordered them to reconvene at San Carlos and address the issues delineated by their commander. The court-martial transcripts of Kid, Askisaylala, Nahconquisay, Margey, and Bachoandoth were returned to Mills "for reconsideration of the sentence in each case."[15]

In his instructions, General Miles made it clear that after reviewing the transcripts he did not accept their findings or their sentence. Based on the facts in these cases General Miles felt that "he would not be justified" in accepting their recommendations. In his instructions Miles immediately went to the heart of the issue. He explained that although the prisoners were scouts enlisted in the U.S. Army, it seemed clear that they were "ignorant, unlettered Indians" who could not speak to members of the court without using two interpreters speaking English, Spanish, and Apache languages. Miles noted that these scouts were not wearing military uniforms, and they were acting under the direction of Al Sieber, a civilian chief of scouts. Further, they had not been instructed in military rules of conduct and were unaware of the nature or the significance of the Articles of War. They were unfamiliar with military discipline, uninformed as to their responsibilities as soldiers, and still fraternizing freely and regularly with their fellows in the SI band, "sharing its sympathies and participating in its customs and ceremonies."[16] This comment by Miles indicates that he understood the predicament of the scouts. He realized that they were Apaches first and scouts second; therefore, it would be unfair to judge them under the same criteria as those applied to regular soldiers.

In his orders to the court-martial panel General Miles explained that after accompanying the SI band to execute the system of summary punishment still practiced among the Apaches, the five scouts had returned to surrender at San Carlos. Miles noted Antonio Díaz's warning to them that they would be banished to Florida if they did not obey orders, that all five scouts had stated that they heard this announcement, and that it had been corroborated by the testimony of their chief, Gonshayee. Miles was convinced that this declaration provoked other members of Kid's SI band to open fire on the tent. Miles concluded that the prisoners had been perfectly obedient, had surrendered their arms and belts, and were about to head for the guardhouse as ordered. The commanding officer also noted that Captain Pierce, who had just disarmed them, claimed that there were no hostile indications from them and that he heard no exclamations from the defendants about putting up a fight nor did he see any hostile acts on the part of any of the scouts. Miles concluded that the evidence was conclusive despite Díaz's testimony to the contrary. In his opinion, the facts proved that the only ones to fire their weapons were SI band members who believed that the scouts would be sent to Florida. In the tumult that followed Díaz's pronouncement, the prisoners decided "to fly at all hazards rather than to submit to banishment."[17] Clearly, Miles understood that Díaz's statement was enough evidence to indicate that the Apache scouts had not mutinied.

After examining Lieutenant Baldwin's challenges, General Miles articulated his belief that the actions of the scouts were, indeed, serious and might have been subversive of discipline. Nevertheless, the scouts were not guilty of participating in a "willful and premeditated mutiny." Therefore, he decided that their actions were not of such extreme gravity as to justify the death sentence. However, Miles explained that these men should be judged exclusively under the military code. Here Miles separated military from civil law when he observed that although they went on a raid that included some depredations when they left the reservation, the SI band members, not the scouts, would probably be held accountable by the civil authorities, who most likely would issue formal criminal complaints against them. Miles informed the panel that during their deliberations they must not hold these civil law issues against the defendants and must not be biased by these facts. Once again, he reminded them that they were trying the scouts strictly for military crimes. Therefore, he explained that the sentences were excessive and the panel must reassemble and reevaluate their findings and sentences.[18]

The court-martial panel reconvened at Fort Thomas and began their deliberations, using Miles's recommendations as their guidelines. After consideration the court-martial panel revoked their first sentence and submitted a revised one ordering that all of the defendants be confined at hard labor for the rest of their lives. After reaching this new verdict on August 6, 1887, they forwarded it to General Miles. After further evaluation, on December 27, 1887, General Miles used his powers of mitigation to reduce the life sentences to ten years in prison.

On January 23, 1888, the Adjutant General of the Army ordered that the Apache scout prisoners be transported to the federal military prison at Alcatraz to serve their sentences. Under armed guard they were conveyed by stagecoach and railroad to San Francisco, arriving there after a three-day journey. Because the records for military prisoners on Alcatraz are no longer extant, we know virtually nothing about Kid's confinement on the Rock. In 1853 the federal government had put huge gun emplacements on the island and labeled it Fort Alcatraz. In 1868 it became a federal prison to house military prisoners. During the late nineteenth century Native Americans treated as war prisoners were sentenced to serve time at Alcatraz. Slosux and Brancho, involved in the Modoc War in northern California, were imprisoned there in 1873. Few Indians survived this type of hard confinement, and many died of consumption, as did Brancho in May 1875. Slosux survived his confinement and was released two years later.[19] Kid was not the first Apache scout to visit Alcatraz. At least two others, privates 15 and 19, were convicted by court-martial for mutiny at Cibecue in 1881 and were sentenced to hard labor. In 1884 General George Crook had sent Kayatennae, a young Chiricahua chief, to Alcatraz for punishment. Apparently, Kayatennae had become "thoroughly reconstructed" by his experience. The general concluded that "his stay at Alcatraz has worked a complete reformation of his character"; as a reward Crook hired him as a scout.[20]

In some ways, physically and psychologically, Alcatraz paralleled the conditions that existed at San Quentin, California's first state prison, located only a few miles further north in the Marin County area. Conditions in such prisons were quite primitive, with minimal ventilation and light. Most cell blocks suffered from overcrowding, and prison authorities often assigned two to four prisoners to a cell. The exact dimensions of the cellblocks at Alcatraz are unknown, but San Quentin's Stones' cells were five feet eleven inches by nine feet ten inches. Instead of housing a single inmate in each cell, the Stones held four without adequate ventilation, light, or sanitary facilities. Punishment of prisoners who violated rules could be quite severe, with floggings of up to 150 lashes with a whip, and prison officials developed the most horrific types of "reforms," which included the use of the dungeon or dark cell. Solitary confinement in dark cells caused a great deal of emotional trauma for the inmates and no doubt, if they broke prison rules, Kid and his fellow Apache scouts probably suffered similar treatment at Alcatraz.[21]

Although General Miles had reviewed and modified the sentences of Kid and his scouts, the review process had to pass through another stage. Next, Lieutenant Tyson, the judge advocate, sent the full transcript of the court-martial to the Judge Advocate General's Department in

Apache Kid in handcuffs, 1888. Courtesy Arizona State Library,
Archives and Public Records, History and Archives Division, Phoenix, #97-6651

Washington, D.C., for further consideration. Every general court-martial had to be filed and reviewed before the legal procedure could be completed. This review process is, indeed, one of the strengths of the military court system. According to regulations, Judge Advocate General Lieber or another member of his legal staff had to evaluate the entire process of the court-martial. Lieutenant Baldwin, defense counsel, had challenged members of Kid's court-martial panel, and now Lieber had these challenges and the full transcript in hand as he began his review.

In order to ensure the legal rights of the defendant, Article 88 specified that any or all court-martial panel members may be challenged by the prisoner, and defense counsel had to state his reasons. The process of challenging court-martial panel members, although not the same, might be compared with challenging jurors in our criminal justice system. The main difference is that during a trial the judge controls the *voir dire*, the method of challenging jurors. Consequently, with the *voir dire* an impartial judge acts as the mediator between the prosecution and the defense to determine which prospective jurors will be accepted to sit on the jury panel. With the court-martial system, however, the members challenged are actually being judged by their fellow panel members, which suggests a conflict of interest and a lack of fairness to the defendant. With eight officers holding similar views it is not difficult to imagine why they might vote to keep other members on the panel despite challenges of bias and prejudice toward the defendants.

Normally the challenge process would occur after the specifications of charges were read to the accused and the names of the court members were detailed by the judge advocate. At that time the defendant or his counsel was required to present their objections. These challenges might be made either orally or in writing, and they were treated as a legal procedure completely separate from the actual court-martial. Usually defense counsel would challenge the court member by oral examination, similar to a *voir dire*, to determine whether there was evidence of bias or prejudice against the defendant. After the defense counsel made his charges and oral arguments, the room would be cleared of everyone, including the challenged member, while the remaining court members deliberated on whether the challenge should be sustained. A majority vote was required to sustain a challenge. If it was not sustained, the challenged member returned and resumed his seat on the court-martial panel. If sustained, the challenged member would be excused from the court.[22]

Defense counsel challenged court members for a variety of reasons, including forming or expressing opinions, holding prejudice or hostility toward the defendant, or being a material witness to the alleged offense. To constitute valid cause, any opinion had to be on the question of guilt or innocence. An opinion expressed by the challenged court member necessarily disqualified him; however, the opinion need not have been expressed openly if it had been fully formed in the mind. In regards to alleged personal prejudice or hostility, such a challenge would be sustained by proof of language or conduct on the part of the member that indicated a decidedly unfavorable estimate of the accused or bias against him. Prejudice could be implied from the relationship of the panel member with the "subject-matter of the charge." Consequently, personal animosity exhibited or entertained against the defendant was commonly held to constitute grounds for a challenge to be sustained.[23]

On January 17, 1888, Lieber received the full trial transcripts of the five Apache scouts convicted of mutiny and desertion and began his legal review. In his appeals brief, Lieber thoroughly discussed the charges of mutiny and desertion against the five defendants and noted that they had been gone for twenty-five days before they returned and surrendered. Lieber noted that Lieutenant Baldwin had challenged several of the court members. Beginning with the first challenge Lieber meticulously examined this legal process that revealed the bias of the court-martial panel members against the defendant.

First, Lieutenant Baldwin had challenged Captain Alpheus H. Bowman and asked him if he had "formed or expressed any opinion concerning the acts or conduct of the accused." Bowman testified that he was a witness "to what occurred" on June 1, 1887. Asked whether he harbored any bias or prejudice toward the defendant, Bowman said: "No. As a member of this Court I have not." The room was cleared of all parties to the court-martial, including Captain Bowman, and, after deliberations, the challenge was not sustained.[24] As noted earlier, Bowman had watched the five scouts surrender to Captain Pierce; he must have formed some opinions that would have been inimical to Kid. Baldwin knew this, but the court-martial panel still did not sustain the challenge. This is an important point; it reveals that the panel by its first vote had become a unified body of army officers who thought alike and acted in unison on this case.

Baldwin then called Captain Robert G. Smither and asked whether he held any bias toward the accused. Smither admitted that he had "some biased opinions" about the actions of the defendant. Despite this he claimed to be satisfied that he held no ill feelings toward Kid and that he had said nothing to prevent himself from being fair to the accused. He admitted, however, that he "saw at a distance what occurred." Smither contended: "I have fully determined to remove from my mind or thoughts anything that had previously occurred and be guided solely on the evidence that might be submitted." This challenge also was not sustained.[25]

Defense objected to Lieutenant Hayden DeLany and asked him if he held any bias toward the defendant. DeLany responded: "No. Not that I can remember." Asked if he had determined the guilt of Kid, DeLany said: "I have." Baldwin explained to him that under oath, "when any doubt arises [the court member] determines according to his understanding and therefore if at any time you have expressed opinions inimical to the accused, would not that doubt be influenced by previous opinions?" DeLany still claimed that he had heard no evidence on the case and felt that he was "perfectly able to try the accused." How could someone who believed that the defendant was guilty still think that he could distance himself from the issues and be impartial? The challenge was not sustained.[26]

Baldwin challenged Lieutenant Carter Johnson, alleging that he had "already formed and expressed an opinion as to the guilt of the accused." Johnson was an important witness because he had led the main pursuit group in an attempt to capture Kid and his raiding party. After he had returned to San Carlos, not surprisingly, Johnson had expressed opinions on the nature of the punishment for Kid. In other words, he had already assumed the guilt of the defendant. Baldwin questioned whether he was in "any way biased, prejudice or inimical against the accused." Johnson answered: "No." Then Baldwin asked: "Are you the officer who recently pursued and drove a party of Indians back to this reservation?" Johnson said he was. He also stated that he had heard the name of one Indian who had been involved in the June 1, 1887, disturbance. Johnson believed Kid was in this group of Apaches, and he admitted that he "may have expressed an opinion on several occasions to that effect." Johnson acknowledged that he also had expressed opinions about Kid during his seventeen days of trailing them across southern Arizona. Questioned whether his opinions had been prejudiced toward Kid, Johnson replied: "An officer following a public enemy can scarcely be supposed to be friendly to him, provided he proposes to do his duty when he overtakes him." He still felt that such feeling "might easily cease to exist" if the renegades came back and voluntarily surrendered. After Baldwin asked if he had formed any opinions about the type of punishment that should be applied to Kid, Johnson replied: "I did." Johnson testified: "I have stated that all my opinions have been based on rumors more or less authentic and not on facts . . . to the best of my knowledge and belief. I can conceive of no prejudice against the accused in person." The challenge was not sustained.[27] Johnson's testimony seems blatantly biased. By this time Lieber must have seen the well-developed pattern of bias that existed against Kid.

Baldwin asked Lieutenant James B. Hughes whether he held any bias or prejudice against this defendant. Hughes answered that he did not. Hughes admitted that he had "formed but expressed no opinion" as to the guilt of Kid. Baldwin: "Have you at any time believed the accused to be guilty of the acts alleged against the accused?" Hughes: "I have."

Under further questioning, Hughes testified that he had discussed the case with other officers and knew the crimes that Kid had been charged with. Baldwin asked Hughes whether his mind was free of any ill feelings or prejudice. Hughes replied: "As the accused is one among a number whom I believe guilty of the offenses with which he is charged, my mind is not free of bias or prejudice." During cross-examination the judge advocate asked whether his bias or prejudice would prevent him from doing justice to the accused. Hughes said, "No." Baldwin: "Please explain how being biased and prejudiced against the accused that you can divest your mind thereof and render judgment impartially and decide upon a question of guilty or innocence, when that fact may only be determined by resolving a doubt in your mind for or against the accused?" Hughes testified that he could "form an opinion solely from evidence" in this case despite his previous belief or knowledge about Kid.[28] The challenge was not sustained.

Finally, Baldwin challenged Lieutenant William G. Elliot for forming and publicly expressing opinions about the accused. Asked whether he had expressed prejudicial opinions about the guilt of the accused, Elliot answered that he had. When asked what those opinions were, Elliot admitted that, although absent when the events occurred, he had asked questions about the participants and had been told that Kid and other scouts had been charged with mutiny and desertion. Upon hearing this, he denounced the defendants and "talked about it as a matter of public notoriety." Asked who had told him about the participants, Elliot testified that he had received a telegram from Captain Pierce. Questioned if he believed the accused was guilty and whether he could try this case without bias or prejudice against Kid, Elliot replied, "Yes." The challenge was not sustained. That ended Baldwin's challenges of the original members of the court-martial panel. Not one of them was sustained.[29] After examining Baldwin's challenges Lieber must have recognized the bias and prejudice held by these six court members against Kid.

When the court-martial continued after the challenges had been completed, Captain Bowman, a panel member, asked to make a statement to the court. Bowman: "Referring to my reply of yesterday on being challenged on grounds of bias . . . I deem it proper to say, before the Court proceeds further, that on mature reflection I have grave doubts that I could vote on the findings in these cases, giving the prisoners the benefit of any doubt that might have come up in my mind. In others words, I find it difficult to divest myself of a decided bias against the accused." Baldwin again challenged Bowman. After considering the challenge, the judge advocate decided that no action would be taken until the objection issue was resolved by communication with the commanding officer; he would need to resolve the challenge issue. In secret session, the court members directed Judge Advocate Tyson to present the essential facts to General Miles. On June 29, 1887, Tyson sent a telegram to Miles requesting further instructions. Four days later the court reconvened and received the following directions. The commander saw no legal reason why the court should not proceed with the trial. General Miles, however, realized that if the challenge against Bowman was sustained, and there was no reason to believe that it would not be, that would reduce the panel to five members, the bare minimum required to continue the court-martial proceedings. Consequently, Miles ordered Major Mills and Lieutenants Hunt and Read, three additional court members, to proceed to San Carlos to guard against the possibility that one of the members might become ill and would have to be excused. The court reconvened and, after reconsidering the objections to Captain Bowman, asked the challenged member to withdraw from the court.[30] Although six officers had expressed bias against Kid, only one, Captain Bowman, had the moral strength to admit that he could not be fair. This was a courageous act on his part; he was going against the grain of a consensus view that military law was about punishment, not the protection of a defendant's rights.

This stage of the court-martial procedure may appear to be flawed; however, under military law the panel was allowed to review individual members. As suggested earlier, the solidarity of the officers on the panel was quite apparent. It is most likely that these officers subscribed to the traditional school of military law that believed punishment must be harsh and quickly applied, especially for the crimes of mutiny and desertion. There is little doubt that they shared similar opinions on military law and discipline to be applied to anyone who violated the rules and that they were well aware of and may have discussed the mutiny at Cibecue only six years before that had ended in disaster when Captain Hentig and seven enlisted men were killed. Accordingly, they would be likely to view Kid and his scouts as a dangerous threat to military authority. Mutiny was an officer's worst nightmare. Considering those dramatic events, why shouldn't these officers stand together as a band of military brothers in order to send a message that such behavior would not be tolerated in the U.S. Army and that punishment would be swift and severe? Nevertheless, they could not run roughshod over the rights of the accused.

After examining the challenges and General Miles's legal comments, Judge Advocate General Lieber carefully reviewed the full transcripts that he had received from Lieutenant Tyson. The reviewing officer began his analysis of the court-martial of Kid by noting that all of the officers except Lieutenant Carter Johnson had been stationed at San Carlos. Lieber observed that, given the testimony of these officers, "it is evident that the members challenged, although disavowing any bias or prejudice against the prisoners," had formed opinions as to the guilt of the five scouts. Their opinions must have become operational as soon as the prisoners were connected with the events that occurred at San Carlos. Lieber noted that their preconceived opinions were "not consistent with the rights of the prisoners to a fair and impartial trial."[31] After examining all five cases, Lieber counseled that "we cannot escape from considering them in passing upon the question whether or not the prisoners had a fair and impartial trial." Lieber explained that all of the charges that had been made against Kid were used in the trials of the other scouts and did "not materially differ." While discussing the events presented in Kid's court-martial, Lieber commented that during the disturbance about fifteen or twenty shots were fired. When the commotion began at least two members of the mounted Indians observing the surrender had raised their guns up and fired. Lieber noted that Sayes, one of these Apaches, was from "the same band as four of the prisoners."[32]

Lieber explained that General Miles had carefully weighed the evidence and had drawn "logical conclusions" that, considering the circumstances and evidence, the trial was unfair. Lieber concurred with General Miles's conclusions that the prisoners were ignorant Indians who did not understand the court-martial proceedings and that Antonio Díaz most likely made the statement about the scouts' being banished to Florida. Although there was some disagreement whether the defendants had made hostile comments, Lieber explained that Captain Pierce had testified that "he heard no exclamation nor saw any act of hostility on the part of any of the scouts." Further, Lieber argued that the evidence was rather conclusive that the Indians on horseback watching the surrender fired the shots, not the scouts. Lieber finally recommended that since the trials were not fair ones and the evidence failed to sustain the findings, the sentences should be remitted.[33] With the Judge Advocate General having remitted his sentence, Kid might have expected his legal ordeal to have come to an end, but the process was not yet complete, and he was in for another disappointment.

At this stage of the review Lieber was required to send his recommendations to the secretary of war, the final reviewing officer in these particular court-martial cases. On April 11, 1888, Lieber delivered his findings to Secretary of War W. C. Endicott. Two days later, Endicott's secretary sent the following message to Lieber: "As these Indians have been in confinement such a short time, the Secretary of War will take no action at present, but desires to have the matter laid before him again six months hence."[34] After both General Miles and Lieber, in their legal briefs, had found the scouts not guilty of the charges against them, and since they already had been incarcerated for a year, it seems remarkable that

Secretary of War Endicott, with a law degree from Harvard, ordered them to be confined for at least an additional six more months. The legal nature of the cases may not have been the main issue; perhaps Endicott shared Sherman's view that military law should be used to punish. Maybe Endicott felt that the Apache scouts deserved more severe punishment for their actions; after all, they were only Indians who needed to cool off for a while at Alcatraz. However, considering the legal reviews submitted by Miles and Lieber, justice was not served in these cases. Sadly, Endicott's arbitrary decision reveals that the whole military legal process seemed to be a mockery of justice.

Some might question whether Kid received due process during his trial. Defendants under courts-martial, although not protected by Article III of the U.S. Constitution or the Fifth Amendment, were accorded the right of due process under military law. For civilians due process is guaranteed by the Fifth Amendment, which states, "No person shall be held to answer for a capital . . . crime, unless on presentment or indictment of a Grand Jury, except in cases arising in the land or naval forces."[35] The Fifth Amendment also provides protection from double jeopardy and self-incrimination and the right to due process. The amendment, however, exempts the military from these protections. Various military legal cases have been argued before the U.S. Supreme Court in regard to these protections under the Fifth Amendment. For example, in an opinion delivered in *Johnson v. Sayre* (1895) Justice Horace Gray explained to the respondent's attorney that military personnel were not granted protection under the Fifth Amendment, and since the defendant had received a copy of the charges filed against him as required by the Articles of War, he had received due process as recognized in military law.[36] In *Reaves v. Ainsworth* (1911) Justice Joseph McKenna argued: "Besides, what is due process of law must be determined by circumstances. To those in the military or naval service of the United States the military law is due process. The decision, therefore, of a military tribunal acting within the scope of its lawful powers cannot be reviewed or set aside by the courts."[37]

In the nineteenth century due process under military law included the following rights: the defendant must receive a copy of the charges against him, have the ability to challenge members of the court, not be held for more than eight days before the trial, have legal representation provided either by the judge advocate or a court-appointed military officer or attorney, be provided with witnesses of his own choosing for his defense, have the ability to cross-examine witnesses, and, finally, be allowed to testify or make a statement on his own behalf. It seems clear that Kid was accorded all of these rights; he did receive due process as provided by the Articles of War and all subsequent laws passed for their enforcement.

As instructed, in late October Lieber returned the cases of the five scouts to the secretary of war for further consideration. In return, John Tweedle, personal secretary to the secretary of war, dispatched this brief note to Lieber: "The unexpired portions of the sentences of the within named Indians will be remitted." Two weeks later General O. O. Howard, Commander of Headquarters, Division of the Pacific, San Francisco, requested authority to return the five Apache scouts to San Carlos.[38] In an unusual turn of events, according to Edward Arhelger, the agency blacksmith, in early November upon their return to San Carlos, Kid and his four Apache scouts were "serenaded" by the Tenth Cavalry band as they entered the camp.[39] Despite this brief musical interlude, their return was met with a great deal of hostility by military officers and civilian employees at San Carlos, who believed that the scouts should have been punished severely. To them it was a miscarriage of justice that the five scouts convicted of mutiny could be released so easily.

Upon his return Kid quickly discovered that there was indeed strong sentiment to find a way to punish him more severely. San Carlos authorities chose to press charges against him by using both federal and territorial court authority. In November 1888 Captain Bullis, San Carlos Indian

Apache Kid and codefendants at Globe, Arizona, 1889. Apache Kid is second from the right in the back row. Courtesy Arizona State Library, Archives and Public Records, History and Archives Division, Phoenix, #96-3660

agent, filed a complaint against Kid and ordered his arrest. The U.S. attorney for the U.S. District Court, Second District, charged Kid with the murder of Michael Grace near Crittenden during the raid the previous year. On November 17, 1888, just a few days after his return from Alcatraz, Kid was arrested, transported to Tucson, and incarcerated in the Pima County jail to await arraignment. After the murder charges were presented against him on March 4, 1889, Kid was bound over to await a grand jury hearing. Although Miguel probably had killed Grace, federal authorities apparently believed that since Kid had led the raiding party, they could make their case against him. The following month, the U.S. Supreme Court ordered the release of Gonshayee because he had been illegally tried by federal authorities instead of the Arizona territorial county courts.[40] This decision meant that the U.S. district court lacked authority to try Kid for murder, and he was released from custody.

In October 1889 Gila County District Attorney J. D. McCabe, no doubt pressured by Sieber and Captain Bullis, filed a complaint in the Arizona Territorial District Court, Gila County, against Kid for assault with intent to murder the chief of scouts. Clearly, the charges against him were contrived simply to prosecute and convict him. It was an attempt by both military and civilian authorities to get even by punishing Kid for a crime he did not commit; it would be difficult to find a more capricious legal system. This bewildering turn of events further illuminates the state of legal confusion about Indians and their legal rights in the nineteenth-century American West. Unknowingly, Bullis had set in motion the final transformation of Kid into a renegade.

On October 29, 1889, Judge Joseph H. Kibbey presided in the case against Kid, with the prosecution calling Al Sieber, Frank Porter, Vacasheviejo, and Fred Knipple to testify against the defendant. All prosecution witnesses except Vacasheviejo held a great deal of enmity and prejudice against Kid. With Merijilda Grijalva acting as interpreter, Kid asked to testify on his own behalf, and E. H. Cook and Mills Van Wagenen, court-appointed defense counsel, also called Nasahasay (Beauty), Tony, and Notlishsay to testify. Whether Nasahasay was Kid's wife is unknown. Unfortunately, there is no transcript of the trial extant and only minimal coverage in the newspapers, so we can only speculate on what took place in the Gila County courthouse in Globe. Sieber, Porter, and Knipple provided enough testimony, perjured or otherwise, to make this bogus charge stick.

This raises the question: Why did Sieber testify for the prosecution for a crime that he knew Kid did not commit? Sieber could have been a friendly witness; instead, he chose to testify against Kid and assured that Kid would be convicted. As noted earlier, Wharfield concluded that Sieber and Kid may not have been close; the civilian scout's testimony supports that hypothesis. Although working for Sieber, Kid had been hired over a five-year period by army officers who made the scout assignments. Kid, under the command of an officer, was required to obey military law. On the other hand, Sieber remained a civilian scout who could not be punished by military law. It is possible that Sieber had difficulty controlling his scouts and also may have been somewhat jealous of their status. As enlisted men the Apache scouts received an extra thirteen dollars a month to maintain their horses. One contemporary author, Dan Williamson, heard Al Sieber say that "Kid's downfall was more misunderstanding than criminal intention."[41] It seems odd that Sieber would say this when he and Captain Bullis were responsible for the unfair prosecution of Kid. Whatever the reasons for Sieber's testimony, Kid suffered at the hands of civilian authorities in his final trial.

Edward Arhelger, an observer of the brief legal proceedings, stated that Kid was "promptly found guilty, which I think myself was wrong, but the sentiment was such that a good Indian was a dead Indian."[42] It should be noted that technically this was not double jeopardy, because the charges against Kid were for different crimes tried in separate legal jurisdictions, military and civil. As Winthrop explained it, an "officer or a soldier may be brought to trial both by a court-martial" for any offense against the Articles of War and also "by a civil tribunal for the civil crime."[43] Considering the treatment of other Apache defendants, it should not be surprising to learn that the trial lasted less than a day. Kid, along with Bachoandoth, Hale, and Sayes, his three codefendants, and four other Apaches charged with other crimes were all found guilty. Judge Kibbey sentenced Kid to serve seven years in the Arizona Territorial Prison.[44] In an interesting twist of fate, about two weeks earlier, in another criminal case involving some of the SI band members who had fled with Kid, Askisaylala and Nahconquisay, two of the scouts involved in the mutiny, along with Gonshayee, had been convicted of murdering William Diehl in Pinal County during their 1887 raid. All were sentenced to death and ordered to be hanged in Florence, Arizona.[45] Through his decision to leave his duty post and enforce Apache social customs of retribution, Kid had brought down the full force of the criminal justice system upon himself and six fellow SI band members.

*

The Arizona Territorial criminal justice system was controlled by whites, many of whom perceived Apaches as a threat. Indians, who could nei- ther vote nor serve on juries, lived virtually unprotected. In 1883, while discussing justice, Robert G. Ingersoll observed: "We must remember that we have to make judges out of men, and that by being made judges their prejudices are not diminished and their intelligence is not increased."[46] In an address delivered January 17, 1899, Oliver Wendell Holmes suggested that one of the "gravest defects [of juries is] . . . that they will introduce into their verdict a certain amount—a very large amount, so far as I have observed—of popular prejudice, and thus keep the administration of the law in accord with the wishes and feelings of the community."[47] The views of these two judges on juries may help to explain what happened to Kid.

Clifford Geertz proposes that both law and ethnography operate under the "local knowledge" created within a particular society. Geertz believes that "legal facts" are "socially constructed . . . by everything from evidence rules, courtroom etiquette, and law reporting traditions, to advocacy, techniques, [and] the rhetoric of judges." This raises serious questions for the administration of justice when two or more cultures interact. Geertz concludes that "if law differs, from this place to that, this time to that, this people to that, what it sees does as well."[48] Consequently, whether it be white or Apache local knowledge, its devel- opment and meaning is quite different within each society. Therefore, in the legal realm each cultural group operates under the dictates of its own local knowledge. In Kid's legal predicament we are dealing with two, sometimes three, legal systems: military and civil authorities failed to understand that the "facts" surrounding his behavior were culturally determined and that his actions took place within a culture very differ- ent from the system that they understood. They never took into consid- eration the Apache social customs in their treatment of Kid. Both military and civilian authorities tried him and held him to the standards of white social, legal, and moral values. Consequently, the "facts" of the case were never understood to be the same from the perspectives of the courts and Kid. In Arizona there were three legal systems operating from three different perspectives. During the events leading up to the legal drama surrounding him, Kid's actions were based upon an Apache perspective. Thereafter, the events, rules, politics, social customs, beliefs, sentiments, symbols, and procedures that led to the killing of Rip were viewed differently by both military judge advocates and civil lawyers. There is no evidence to suggest that either the military or civil authorities ever made any attempts to deal with the cultural wall that separated them from the Apaches.

Finally, it seems clear that Kid could not have received a fair trial in either the military or civil law systems in Arizona Territory. Although released by the army with the remission of his sentence, Kid had been incarcerated for two years under intolerable conditions in the San Carlos Guardhouse, Alcatraz Prison, and the Pima and Gila county jails. Research reveals that the nineteenth-century death rates for Indian inmates in Yuma Territorial and San Quentin prisons were 37 and 44 percent, respectively.[49] Kid and his fellow scouts were fortunate to have survived these primitive penal facilities. Without the devotion to fair treatment exhibited by Miles, Lieber, and Baldwin, however, Kid could have died in Alcatraz as did many other Indians, including Apache scouts. Instead, he had survived his ordeal.

EPILOGUE

RENEGADE

Tombstone, Arizona, May 9.—A band of renegade Apaches under
the leadership of "The Kid" are on the warpath near the Mexican
line. . . . The renegades a month or so ago made a murderous in-
cursion from Old Mexico and crossed the frontier before United
States troops arrived.

New York Times, May 10, 1896

.   .   .

This newspaper headline portrayed Kid as a dangerous man who
raided across the border any time he wanted to. The term *renegade*
has generally been used to identify anyone who has deserted either a
group or a principle in favor of another. *Renegade* evokes a negative con-
notation and in this case refers to a defiant Apache who had challenged
white authorities.[1] As noted earlier, Kid, after enlisting and serving five
years as an Apache scout and escaping civil custody, had turned against
the military in order to survive as a fugitive. He had become an outcast,
apparently reviled by Apache and white alike. Military authorities commonly used *renegade* as a label for Geronimo, Victorio, Juh, Nana,
Massai, and any other Apaches who left the reservation. Four years earlier, General A. McD. McCook defined Kid as an outlaw fleeing from
civil authorities, and two years later Captain Albert L. Myers, the new
Indian agent at San Carlos, referred to him as "the renegade," suggesting
that he was extremely dangerous.[2] Military authorities believed that Kid,

serving as an Apache scout, had bought into the civilian and military complex that had been imposed upon Indians in the Arizona Territory: Kid had betrayed them. They had offered him "the good life" as a first sergeant of scouts, and then he suddenly had turned against them. Consequently, they saw him as the worst sort of renegade who deserved to be hunted down and eliminated. On the other hand, Kid, after existing within the liminal world between Indian and white cultures for more than five years, had been forced by a series of unusual events to revert back to his Apache roots. In 1892, just two years after his daring escape, Apache Kid had joined the ranks of the lawless elements in the Arizona Territory by making another of his daring raids across the border from Mexico onto the San Carlos reservation.

A year later, ten detachments of U.S. cavalry and infantry troops searching for the fugitive were unable to see let alone capture him. Since Kid always eluded his pursuers, his exploits made for hot news coverage that tended toward exaggeration. As a renegade, Kid became the Apache challenger to white domination and authority, the much-feared red avenger, a compelling historical figure, larger than life, who fought and defeated the white man at every turn in a fashion similar to that of Nana or Ulzana. This former scout, however, fought alone. In an era that witnessed disastrous assaults by whites on Apaches and the decline of Apache society and culture, a time that left many Apaches locked up on barren reservations and morally devastated, Kid became the heroic symbol of Apache resistance. Even worse, from the perspective of the Arizona territorial government, Kid remained on the loose and became ubiquitous—the undefeated, a real or imagined threat to white society. Whether viewed as a fugitive from justice or as a renegade, by the end of the nineteenth century he would become an Arizona legend. Kid had, indeed, become what his detractors called "the renegade of renegades"; however, he was not the only fugitive on the loose in Arizona.

*

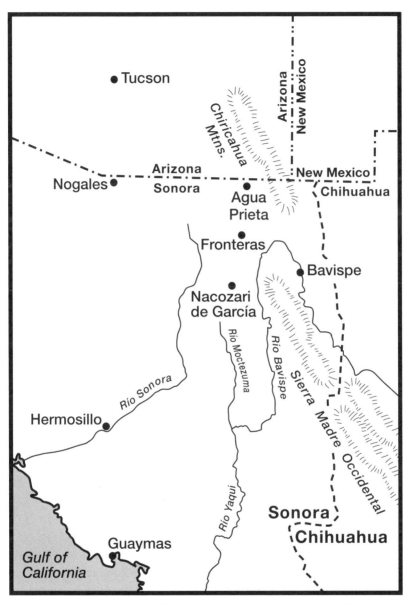

Kid's Sierra Madre stronghold in Mexico, about 1889. Courtesy Melodie Tune, graphic artist, Instructional Technology Services, San Diego State University

Massai, Apache Kid, and Rowdy, Apache scouts, 1885. Courtesy Arizona State Library, Archives and Public Records, History and Archives Division, Phoenix, #97-2603

Massai, a Chiricahua scout, also had turned against whites who had mistreated him. On November 7, 1885, when he had enlisted as a scout at Fort Apache under the command of Lieutenant Marion Maus, Massai was listed as thirty-eight years of age and five feet eight inches tall. He served with Kid under the command of Captain Emmet Crawford during the Geronimo campaign when General Crook's troops invaded the Sierra Madre in Mexico. His career as a scout, however, was short-lived, and he was discharged on May 6, 1886.[3] He was a Chiricahua, and soon after his discharge he and all the rest of the Chiricahua scouts were arrested, placed on a train with Geronimo and his band, and transported to Florida for internment. As the train passed through Missouri, Massai saw his chance, jumped off, and began the long walk back to Arizona. Now a very angry man, upon his return he began to conduct raids in New Mexico and Arizona, taking out his frustrations on any white settlers or Apaches who resisted his attacks. On October 26, 1889, Mills Van Wagenen, Gila County deputy district attorney, indicted Massai for murdering Sabino Quiroz. The warrant was never served, and during the following years Massai developed a style of raiding that paralleled the tactics of Kid.[4]

Using the oral tradition of Alberta Begay, the daughter of Massai, historian Sherry Robinson confirms that Kid and Massai had become acquainted during the 1885 Geronimo campaign and that both were riding with Captain Emmet Crawford's scouts into the Sierra Madre of Mexico. On January 11, 1886, Crawford was shot and killed, probably intentionally, by Mexican troops, mostly conscripts, looking for Apache scalps that brought a sizable bounty from the Sonoran government. The angry scouts, who loved and respected their commander, quickly fired back, killing Major Mauricio Corredor, the Mexican officer who had shot Crawford, and several other Mexican troops as well.[5] An undated photograph, most likely taken in 1885, shows three scouts—Kid, Massai, and Rowdy—standing together near a group of wickiups that were their living quarters at San Carlos. At least three different stories claim Massai had been killed, but none can be verified.[6] For example, in 1896 the *New York Times* reported that Massai had been killed in Southern Arizona by Apache scouts. Before his alleged death, Massai supposedly killed three scouts. There are no reports from the San Carlos Indian agent or any other credible evidence to confirm this claim. All three of the stories of his demise remain mere speculation.[7]

Kid seemed even more elusive than Massai. Numerous reports written by several San Carlos Indian agents bitterly complained about his exploits, and, of course, all were embarrassed to admit that their military pursuit parties were unable to make even visual contact with the fleeing fugitive, let alone catch him. In October 1890 Captain Bullis, who had worked to put Kid in prison, complained of numerous disturbances on the reservation during the year, including the assaults by Massai. Captain Bullis reported that these renegades, during several raids on San Carlos, killed several men who resisted, carried off women captives, terrorized the others, and tried to persuade some to join them. Bullis admitted that many at San Carlos felt insecure; however, he reported that Kid and Massai were the only "bad Indians" still at large.[8]

Two years later Captain Lewis Johnson, the new Indian agent, complained that Kid, an Apache renegade, had committed assaults upon the San Carlos reservation. He allegedly killed a woman of his own tribe and had raped her daughter and another young White Mountain Apache woman. As usual, Kid eluded the vigorous pursuit and attempts by cavalry units and Indian police to capture him. Johnson believed that Kid had friends at San Carlos who were protecting him. The Indian agent said that he was trying to ferret out the guilty parties. He had learned from reliable informants that Kid had been using the Sierra Madre in Sonora, Mexico, as his hideout.[9] On November 12, 1892, General Alexander McD. McCook, the commander in Arizona, reported that his troops had done everything in their power to overtake and capture Kid.[10] To the embarrassment of the various U.S. Army commanders in Arizona, such reports of attempts to apprehend Kid continued for years.

In 1893 Captain Johnson admitted that Kid had made several intrusions upon the reservation. On at least one occasion Kid was accompanied by two Chiricahuas from Sonora, one of whom might have been Massai. Johnson reported that they had killed an inoffensive and unarmed Indian and had taken away two Indian girls. On another occasion Kid kidnaped a young Tonto Apache woman. Despite a reward of five thousand dollars offered by the territorial government, authorities had been unable to apprehend Kid. Johnson complained that Kid had an advantage because he was very cautious and he had a thorough knowledge of the rough and intricate terrain in Arizona as well as Sonora. The Indian agent considered it "exceedingly doubtful that anything but chance, accident, or treachery will effect his capture." Johnson criticized those who had claimed that Kid was a graduate of Carlisle Indian School and assured his superiors that he was an uneducated common Indian.[11]

*

Trailing Apache Kid, 1890. Courtesy Arizona State Library, Archives and Public Records, History and Archives Division, Phoenix, #97-6683

Despite being isolated in the distant desert hinterland of the American southwest, Kid received a great deal of coverage from newspapers, including the *New York Times*. A November 20, 1892, editorial in the *Times* noted that "Kid—the notorious Apache renegade from the White Mountain Reservation"—was allegedly spotted by troops. It is unlikely that the troops even saw the fugitive, and, as usual, they were unable to capture him.[12] General McCook reported that the military units pursuing Kid included four troops of the Second Cavalry, five from the First Cavalry, and one company of Eleventh Infantry. These detachments searching for the fugitive were unable to see their quarry; Kid always eluded his pursuers.[13] The newspapers exaggerated their accounts of Kid's exploits. An August 13, 1893, a *New York Times* headline labeled Kid as "Apache Renegade The Most Bloodthirsty Scoundrel in the Southwest." They claimed that he was trying to outdo the bloody exploits of Victorio, and, despite his reputation, they admiringly described him as tall and handsome for an Indian. They reported that Kid was a thinker with a peculiar magnetism that had drawn all the scouts of Company A around him as their leader.[14] The *New York Times* editor noted that Kid was not a Carlisle Indian as previously reported. He had never attended school and was unable to read or write. His masterful skills in woodcraft, scouting, and trailing, however, made him formidable and dangerous. The editor suggested that the best way to eliminate Kid would be "to offer 'head money' on the reservation." The editor believed that Apaches often get homesick and want to return; consequently, some of his friends might decide to kill him on one of these sojourns to San Carlos. In May 1896, in their final article on Kid, the *Times* reported that "a band of renegade Apaches under the leadership of 'The Kid' are on the warpath near the Mexican line."[15] Once again they eluded their pursuers.

From 1889 through 1896 the *New York Times* and numerous Arizona newspapers carried stories describing Kid's exploits. In effect these sensational stories helped to build the legend of Apache Kid. Heavy coverage of this flamboyant figure was to be expected in Arizona, but the *New York Times* reports were somewhat surprising. Many of their stories were sensational, with words such as *renegade, notorious, bloodthirsty, scoundrel, depraved, most dangerous, murderous, a marauder,* and *ruthless* being used to describe Kid. But the *Times* also used a variety of words that suggested a certain admiration for him. They described Kid as handsome, a superior Indian, a thinker, bright and intelligent, a recognized leader, and a superb unrivaled scout who could not be caught despite numerous military expeditions. In a feature story that filled two columns the *New York Times* included an illustration of Kid. It looks nothing like him, but with a rifle, knife, headband, and ammunition belt it does reveal the typical dress of an Apache scout. No doubt such national coverage carried Kid's fame to the eastern seaboard, Europe, and the world. Kid made good copy that sold newspapers. The *Times* helped to create this wily, unconquerable Apache who outlasted Geronimo. Kid truly became legendary with the aid of newspaper coverage that made him ubiquitous.[16]

*

Kid's raids focused on San Carlos reservation, and on occasion he may have worked with Massai and other Chiricahuas from Sonora. He returned to San Carlos on numerous occasions to kidnap women and, possibly, to take retribution against those Apaches whom he viewed as enemies. H. B. Wharfield reported that Kid's main haunts were the Ash Flat country, the Santa Catalina Mountains near Oracle, just north of Tucson, and the Sierra Madre in Mexico.[17] The Ash Flat region is near the northern end of Aravaipa Canyon, where Kid had been born and raised. No doubt this whole region, with rugged mountains and barren desert, provided a safe haven while he made his sorties to San Carlos.

In 1931, while interviewing Apaches near Bylas, Grenville Goodwin heard intriguing stories about Kid's exploits. For example, according to one informant, in 1895 Kid conducted a raid on the San Carlos and Fort Apache reservations with four Chiricahua men, possibly including Massai, who had come up from Mexico to steal Indian girls and women. Near Rice Kid killed a Tonto Apache and kidnaped his wife. Later, as they rode south, an Apache police sergeant, who had assembled his Indian police to ambush the Kid, allegedly allowed them to "ride by unmolested." According to the informant, the angry Indian agent at San Carlos allegedly fired all of the Indian police involved. There is no evidence in the San Carlos reports by the Indian agents to verify this. It seems more like an attempt to build up the invincible Kid, and the scouts, employed as police, were afraid of him. They had good reason to be cautious; dealing with Kid could get them killed.

Neil Goodwin reported that Kid kidnaped Djaokin, a young Apache woman, near Fort Apache in 1895. Another story indicates that as late as 1919 a group of Apaches crossed into Arizona from their Sierra Madre stronghold in Mexico and kidnaped an Apache woman at San Carlos.[18] A variety of sources suggest that Kid continued his raids into Arizona for Apache women but apparently never bothered white women. While discussing Kid, Dan R. Williamson, a contemporary observer, stated: "I do not know of an instance where a white woman or child was molested."[19]

Historian Shelley Bowen Hatfield discovered that both the United

States and Mexico feared Kid's raids. Because of his exploits, in June 1890 Mexico approved a reciprocal crossing agreement that allowed troops from both countries to pursue renegades across the border. Despite this, various raids by Kid continued to plague both sides of the border. In February 1896 Arizona territorial governor Louis Hughes requested permission to allow Arizona lawmen to cross the border in pursuit of Apache Kid. The governor had posted a five-thousand-dollar reward for Kid, "dead or alive." The Mexican government signed another agreement with the United States that was to remain in effect until Kid had been either captured or killed. In September 1896 Archie McIntosh, a scout, suggested to General Miles that, with the aid of five Apache scouts, he could capture Kid. Miles, rather foolishly, endorsed the plan, but McIntosh went on a drinking binge and Miles fired him before he began his expedition.[20]

Sherry Robinson provides some interesting details about Kid and his raids that Eve Ball had collected during oral interviews with Apache informants at San Carlos. Robinson recounted the story that Kid had married one of Eskiminzin's daughters in 1884 or 1885. In March 1890 Captain John Bullis, believing that Eskiminzin had been helping Kid, sent the chief, along with Kid's wife and children and other band members, to Mount Vernon Barracks in Alabama, where they ended up with the Chiricahua exiles. Knowing that his wife was literally being "held hostage" may have provoked Kid to raid San Carlos for women. In an interview George Ester, an Apache informant, said that Al Sieber had framed Apache Kid. Sieber knew that Kid was not the one who had shot him. There is little doubt that the Gila County criminal justice system had railroaded Kid.[21] Although there were numerous attempts to catch him, Apache Kid was as elusive as a ghost. No doubt this sort of imagery helped to turn Kid into an Arizona legend.

What happened to Kid remains a mystery today. There are numerous scenarios about his possible demise. According to Robinson, Mrs. Argo

Watson, Kid's sister, reported that he was still visiting her as late as 1896.[22] In 1899 Colonel Emilio Kosterlitsky, commanding Mexican Rurales in Sonora, Mexico, stated that Apache Kid was still leading "a small and well-behaved band of Apaches in the Sierra Madres." With new supporting evidence, writer Ross Santee speculated that Kid was riding with Pancho Villa's troops in 1915. Lieutenant John H. Healy, Tenth Cavalry, remembered that Joe Adley, one of his Apache scouts and Kid's nephew, said that the renegade was still living in the mountainous region of Sonora, Mexico. In 1924 a band of Apaches from the Sierra Madre had crossed the border on a horse-stealing raid into southwestern New Mexico. When asked by Lieutenant Healy about this raid, Adley responded, "Apache Kid, he alive in Mexico." There were alleged reports as late as 1935 that Kid had "visited old friends at San Carlos."[23] Looking back at the saga of Apache Kid, probably no other figure in Arizona history had amassed such wild speculation about who he really was and what he represented; we still do not know the answer. As Thrapp noted: "The beginning and end of the Apache Kid are shrouded in mystery. Only in the prime of his spectacular life does he stand highlighted on the horizon of southwestern history."[24]

In court-martial testimony Kid admitted that he had killed only one man. Looking back at that remarkable chain of events it seems clear that if Kid had not killed Rip, we would know virtually nothing about him today. He would have slipped through the cracks of history, possibly appearing in a footnote of some history book; he would have been lost to us forever. In retrospect, it seems amazing that Kid, born into a chaotic world, survived court-martial, Alcatraz Prison, and two legal jurisdictions; escaped from custody; and turned into a renegade before he reached the age of thirty. A survivor, Kid had returned to his Apache roots and had lived a dashing, remarkable life. There is no contemporary literature that provides insights into whether Apaches viewed Kid as a symbol of resistance to white culture, but they remembered him. Some of those Apaches may have seen him as a heroic figure. Consequently, they could say that Kid, the renegade of renegades, "*t'ah hidaa*—he still lives."

NOTES

PROLOGUE: APACHE KID

1. Dan Thrapp, *Al Sieber: Chief of Scouts*, 320, 337.

2. Ibid., and *Arizona Weekly Enterprise*, November 9, 1889.

3. *Arizona Weekly Enterprise*, November 9, 1889.

4. Ibid.

5. *Arizona Silver Belt*, November 9, 1889.

6. Ibid., July 26, 1890.

7. *New York Times*, August 3, 1890.

8. Testimony of Tony, first sergeant, Apache scouts, p. 87, "General Court-Martial of First Sergeant Kid, Company A, Indian Scouts," Records Received, 4475, December 27, 1887, Judge Advocate General (Army), RG 153, National Archives.

9. Testimony of Gonshayee, ibid., 107.

10. Grenville Goodwin, *The Social Organization of the Western Apache*, 458–62.

11. Ibid., 476.

12. All Apache words or phrases come from Dorothy Bray, ed., *Western Apache–English Dictionary: A Community-Generated Bilingual Dictionary*.

13. Goodwin, *Social Organization of the Western Apache*, 476, and Morris Opler, *An Apache Life-Way: The Economic, Social, and Religious Institutions of the Chiricahua Indians*, 317.

14. Goodwin, *Social Organization of the Western Apache*, 473–74.

15. Opler, *Apache Life-Way*, 568–69.

16. Goodwin, *Social Organization of the Western Apache*, 577–87.

17. Thrapp, *Al Sieber*, 320–25, and Phyllis de la Garza, *The Apache Kid*, 4. See also Jess G. Hayes, *Apache Vengeance*, and William Sparks, *The Apache Kid: A Bear Fight and Other True Stories of the Old West*.

18. Britton Davis, *The Truth about Geronimo*, 38.

19. H. B. Wharfield, "Footnotes to History: Apache Kid and the Record," *Journal of Arizona History* 6 (1965): 37; see also H. B. Wharfield, *10th Cavalry and Border Fights* (El Cajon, CA: n.p., 1965).

20. Thrapp, *Al Sieber*, 252, 323–24; Thomas Cruse, *Apache Days and After*, 160–66; and Wharfield, "Footnotes to History," 37, 39.

21. Hayes, *Apache Vengeance*, 4.

22. U.S. Army, "Registers of Enlistments in the U.S. Army, Indian Scouts, 1878–1914," No. 394, RG 94, M 233, Roll 71, NA; Wharfield, "Footnotes to History," 38.

23. Robert M. Utley, "The Ordeal of Plenty Horses," *American Heritage: The Magazine of History* 36 (December 1974); Clare V. McKanna, Jr., *White Justice in Arizona: Apache Murder Trials in the Nineteenth Century*, 95–105, 122–23.

24. Testimony of Captain Pierce, p. 51, General Court-Martial of First Sergeant Kid, RG 153, NA; and Goodwin, *Social Organization of the Western Apache*, 169, 181.

25. Thrapp, *Al Sieber*, 341.

CHAPTER 1. SAN CARLOS SCOUTS

1. William Winthrop, *Military Law and Precedents*, 540–41.

2. Ibid., 535–40.

3. *The Military Laws of the United States*, 335–36. See also Clayton D. Laurie, "The Philippine Scouts: America's Colonial Army, 1899–1913," *Philippine Studies* 37 (Second Quarter 1989): 174–91; and Alfred W. McCoy, "The Colonial Origins of Philippine Military Traditions," in *The Philippine Revolution of 1896: Ordinary Lives in Extraordinary Times,* ed. Florentino Rodao and Felice Noelle Rodriguez, 83–124.

4. John G. Bourke, *On the Border with Crook*, 221.

5. Timothy Braatz, *Surviving Conquest: A History of the Yavapai Peoples*, 170–78.

6. Thomas Cruse, *Apache Days and After*, 32.

7. Herman Ten Kate, *Travels and Researches*, 210.

8. Ibid., 211–12.

9. Ibid., 193.

10. Ibid., 201.

11. *Annual Report of the Commissioner of Indian Affairs to the Secretary of the Interior for the Year 1880* (Washington, DC: Government Printing Office, 1880), xxi.

12. J. C. Tiffany, Report on San Carlos Agency, *Annual Report of the Commissioner of Indian Affairs, 1881*, 8.

13. Eve Ball, *Indeh: An Apache Odyssey*, 37.

14. Cruse, *Apache Days*, 186.

15. Britton Davis, *The Truth about Geronimo*, 31.

16. Ibid., 31, 33–34.

17. U.S. Congress, Testimony of Captain F. E. Pierce, October 20, 1885, *Reports of Committees, 1885* (Washington, DC: Government Printing Office, 1886), 127–28.

18. Ibid., 135–38.

19. Ibid., 131–35.

20. Captain John L. Bullis, "Report on San Carlos to the Commissioner of Indian Affairs, August 26, 1889," *Annual Report of the Commissioner of Indian Affairs, 1889*, 122–23.

21. Cruse, *Apache Days*, 40.

22. Harry T. Getty, *The San Carlos Indian Cattle Industry*, 11.

23. Captain Francis Pierce, Report on San Carlos Agency, *Annual Report of the Commissioner of Indian Affairs, 1886*, 258–59.

24. Captain John L. Bullis, Report on San Carlos Agency, *Annual Report of the Commissioner of Indian Affairs, 1888*, 7–8.

25. Bourke, *On the Border with Crook*, 36.

26. Ibid., 36–37.

27. George Crook, *Annual Report of General George Crook, Commanding Officer, U.S. Army, Department of Arizona, September 27, 1883* (Prescott, AZ: n.p., 1883), 11–12.

28. Ibid., 11–13.

29. George Crook, *Resume of Operations against Apache Indians, 1882–1886* (Prescott: n.p., 1886), 4, 177; Letter from Crook to Mr. Welsh, in Dan Thrapp, *General Crook and the Sierra Madre Adventure*, 170–71; Thomas W. Dunlay, *Wolves for the Blue Soldiers: Indian Scouts and Auxiliaries with the United States Army, 1860–90*, 72–78.

30. Charles M. Robinson III, ed., *The Diaries of John Gregory Bourke*, Vol. 1, *November 20, 1872–July 28, 1876*, 182.

31. Charles M. Robinson III, *General Crook and the Western Frontier*, 111, 127, 133–36.

32. Ibid., 133–36, and Bourke, *On the Border with Crook*, 190–91, 196.

33. Robinson, *Diaries of Bourke*, 34.

34. Ibid., 82, and Bourke, *On the Border with Crook*, 210.

35. U.S. Congress, *Medal of Honor, 1863–1968*, 1102, 1104–10.

36. *Above and Beyond: A History of the Medal of Honor from the Civil War to Vietnam*, 77.

37. U.S. Congress, Testimony of General George Crook, October 24, 1885, *Reports of Committees, 1885* (Washington, DC: Government Printing Office, 1886), 146.

38. Ibid., 147.

39. Woodworth Clum, *Apache Agent: The Story of John P. Clum*, 97–98.

40. Testimony of General George Crook, October 24, 1885, 151.

41. Sherry L. Smith, *The View from Officers' Row: Army Perception of Western Indians*, 164.

42. Ibid., 165–66, 168–69.

43. Bourke, *On the Border with Crook*, 203.

44. Dan Thrapp, *Al Sieber: Chief of Scouts*, 245–57.

45. Cruse, *Apache Days*, 167–70; U.S. Army, *Registers of Enlistments U.S. Army, 1798–1914* (Washington, D.C.: National Archives), No. 497; Stanley C. Brown, "Whatever Happened to Joseph McLernon, Killed at the Battle of Big Dry Wash?" *Journal of Arizona History* 39 (Spring 1998): 62–64.

46. Bourke, *On the Border with Crook*, 203.

47. Ibid., 480–81.

48. Peter R. DeMontravel, *A Hero to His Fighting Men: Nelson A. Miles, 1839–1925*, 192–93; Robert Wooster, *Nelson A. Miles and the Twilight of the Frontier Army*, 144–45.

49. Louis Kraft, ed., *Lt. Charles Gatewood and His Apache Wars Memoir*, 136.

50. Ibid., 181–85.

CHAPTER 2. KID'S AMBIGUOUS WORLD

1. Grenville Goodwin, *The Social Organization of the Western Apache*, 393.

2. Ibid., 398, 406.

3. Ibid., 395–96.

4. Sidney L. Harring, *Crow Dog's Case: American Indian Sovereignty, Tribal Law, and United States Law in the Nineteenth Century*, 109–10.

5. Ibid., 121–24.

6. Ibid., 134; *Ex Parte Crow Dog*, 109 U.S. 571–72 (1883); and Michael A. Powell, "Crow Dog and the Issue of Tribal Jurisdiction," in *Law in the Western United States*, ed. Gordon Morris Bakken, 283–90.

7. Title 28, Chapter 4, Government of Indian Country, Sections 2145 and 2146, in *Revised Statutes of the United States, 1873–74* (Washington, DC: Government Printing Office, 1875).

8. Chapter 341, Section 9, Major Crimes Act, Indian Appropriations Act, March 3, 1885, in *The Statutes at Large of the United States of America, from December, 1883, to March 1885* (Washington, DC: Government Printing Office, 1885), 385.

9. *U.S. v. Kagama*, 118 U.S. 383–84 (1886).

10. Clare V. McKanna, Jr., *White Justice in Arizona: Apache Murder Trials in the Nineteenth Century*, 39–56.

11. "Indian Commission," HR 6973, 49th Cong., 1st sess., *Congressional Record* 17, Part 3 (April 7, 1886): H 3197–98.

12. Morris Opler, *An Apache Life-Way: The Economic, Social, and Religious Institutions of the Chiricahua Indians*, 369–70.

13. Thomas H. Kearney and Robert H. Peebles, *Arizona Flora*.

14. Opler, *Apache Life-Way*, 369–70; and Captain John G. Bourke, "Distillation by Early American Indians," *American Anthropologist* 7 (July 1894): 297.

15. Captain F. E. Pierce, Acting Agent, Report on San Carlos Agency, in *Annual Report of the Commissioner of Indian Affairs, 1886* (Washington, DC: Government Printing Office, 1886), 40.

16. J. C. Tiffany, Indian Agent, Report on San Carlos Agency, in *Annual Report of the Commissioner of Indian Affairs, 1881*, 9, 11.

17. Captain John L. Bullis, Report on San Carlos Agency, in *Annual Report of the Commissioner of Indian Affairs, 1889*, 122; Frederick Lloyd, Acting Assistant

Surgeon, USA, *Special Report on Indians at San Carlos Agency, Arizona, February 10, 1883* (San Carlos Agency: n.p.), 6.

18. Britton Davis, *The Truth about Geronimo*, 146.

19. Ibid., 148.

20. Ibid., 145–46.

21. Ibid., 145.

22. John G. Bourke, *On the Border with Crook*, 178.

23. Thomas Cruse, *Apache Days and After*, 97.

24. Ibid., 99–101.

25. Ibid., 105–7, 117–18. See also Charles Collins, *Apache Nightmare: The Battle of Cibecue Creek*.

26. William Winthrop, *Military Law and Precedents*, 86, 101–3, 666–70.

27. Argument by Lieutenant E. F. Willcox in "Court-Martial of Sergeant No. 2 (alias Dead Shot)," Case No. 8, Records Received, 2821, November 30, 1881, RG 153, NA.

28. Legal Opinion of Judge Advocate General David Swaim to Secretary of War Robert Lincoln, December 31, 1881, ibid.

29. President Chester A. Arthur's confirmation of death penalty sentence, in General Court-Martial Order No. 12, Headquarters of the Army, Adjutant General's Office, February 6, 1882, in "Court-Martial of Sergeant No. 2 (alias Dead Shot)," Case No. 8, Records Received, 2821, RG 153, NA; "Articles of War, 1874," *Revised Statutes*, 234; and Cruse, *Apache Days*, 139.

30. Albert B. Reagan, *Notes on the Indians of the Fort Apache Region*, 328–29.

31. Dan L. Thrapp, *Al Sieber: Chief of Scouts*, 322.

32. H. B. Wharfield, "Footnotes to History: Apache Kid and the Record," *Journal of Arizona History* 6 (Spring 1965): 39; *Arizona Silver Belt*, January 1, 1887.

33. Tom Horn, *Life of Tom Horn: Government Scout and Interpreter*, 215.

34. Thrapp, *Al Sieber*, 325.

35. Testimony of Captain Pierce, "General Court-Martial of First Sergeant Kid, Company A, Indian Scouts," Records Received, 4475, December 27, 1887, RG 153, NA, 37.

36. Ibid.

37. Testimony of Kid, ibid., 116–17.

38. Testimony of Captain Pierce, ibid., 37.

39. Opler, *Apache Life-Way*, 332–33, 342.

40. *Arizona Weekly Citizen*, June 11, 1887.

41. Testimony of Vacasheviejo, *U.S. v. Gonshayee*, U.S. District Court, Second Judicial District, Arizona Territory, June 4, 1888 (Phoenix: Arizona State Archives), 14–16.

42. *Arizona Weekly Citizen*, June 11, 1887.

43. Opler, *Apache Life-Way*, 347.

44. Dispatch from Dapray, A.A.A.G., to Commanding Officer, Fort Lowell, June 11, 1887, *Reports of General Nelson Miles, Renegade Indians, June 1887–May 1889, San Carlos Reservation*, NA.

45. *Arizona Weekly Citizen*, June 11, 1887.

46. *New York Times*, June 14, 1887; Dispatch from Major General O. O. Howard to Adjutant General of the Army, June 9, 1887, in *Reports of General Nelson Miles, Renegade Indians, June 1887–May 1889, San Carlos Reservation*, NA.

47. General Nelson A. Miles, *Personal Recollections and Observations of General Nelson A. Miles*, 536.

48. Thrapp, *Al Sieber*, 327–28.

49. Dispatch from General Miles to Commanding Officers in the Field, June 15, 1887, and dispatch from General Howard to Adjutant General of the Army, June 15, 1887, in *Reports of General Nelson Miles, Renegade Indians, June 1887–May 1889, San Carlos Reservation*, NA.

50. Dispatch from General Miles to Lieutenant Johnson, June 18, 1887, ibid.

51. Dispatch from General Miles to Assistant Adjutant General, June 25, 1887, ibid.

52. Dispatch from General Miles to Assistant Adjutant General, July 16, 1887, ibid.

53. Report from General Miles to Assistant Adjutant General, Division of the Pacific, July 16, 1887, in *Annual Report of Brigadier General Nelson A. Miles, U.S. Army, Commanding Department of Arizona, 1887*, 3.

54. Ibid., 4.

CHAPTER 3. MILITARY LAW

1. C. E. Brand, *Roman Military Law* (Austin: University of Texas Press, 1968), 68.

2. *Leges Militares*, in ibid., 149–69.

3. Ibid., 151–53, 163–67.

4. "Code of Articles of King Gustavus Adolphus of Sweden, 1621," in William Winthrop, *Military Law and Precedents*, 907–18.

5. Winthrop, *Military Law*, 19–20.

6. William B. Aycock and Seymour W. Wurfel, *Military Law Under the Uniform Code of Military Justice*, 9–14.

7. William R. Hagan, "Introduction," in Winthrop, *Military Law;* and James Grant Wilson and John Fiske, eds., *Appletons' Cyclopaedia of American Biography* 6, 577.

8. *A Manual for Courts-Martial*, ix–x.

9. "Articles of War, 1874," in *Revised Statutes of the United States, 1873–74*, 236; Donald W. Hansen, "Judicial Functions of the Commander?" *Military Law Review* 41 (July 1968): 13–14.

10. Kermit L. Hall, *The Magic Mirror: Law in American History*, 179–85.

11. Ibid., 190, 198–201, and 229.

12. Oliver Wendell Holmes, Jr., *The Common Law*, 1.

13. Edward F. Sherman, "The Civilianization of Military Law," *Maine Law Review* 22 (January 1970): 4.

14. Senate debate on Articles of War, *Annals of the Congress*, 9th Cong., 1st sess., January 2, 1806 (Washington, D.C.: Gales and Seaton, 1852), 15:326–27.

15. Sherman, "The Civilianization of Military Law," 5.

16. Ibid., 7.

17. Terry W. Brown, "The Crowder-Ansell Dispute: The Emergence of General Samuel T. Ansell," *Military Law Review* 35 (January 1967): 2, 5.

18. Hagan, "Introduction," in Winthrop, *Military Law*.

19. Ibid., 88–90.

20. Ibid., 90.

21. Winthrop, *Military Law*, 50; *Dynes v. Hoover*, 61 U.S. 65 (1857); and *Johnson v. Sayre*, 158 U.S. 118 (1895).

22. See *Ex parte Vallandingham*, 68 U.S. 243 (1863); and *Ex parte Milligan*, 71 U.S. 2 (1866).

23. Winthrop, *Military Law*, 49–54.

24. Ibid., 106, 165, 287, 398, and the U.S. Constitution.

25. *Ex parte Mason*, 105 U.S. 697 (1881).

26. "Articles of War, 1874," in *Revised Statutes of the United States, 1873–74*, 236.

27. Winthrop, *Military Law*, 179–85.

28. Final vote of Congress on the Articles of War, *Annals of the Congress*, 9th Cong., 1st sess., April 10, 1806.

29. "Articles of War, 1874," 237.

30. Winthrop, *Military Law*, 170–74.

31. Ibid., 177, and Article 87 in "Articles of War, 1874," 238.

32. Winthrop, *Military Law*, 174.

33. Ibid.

34. Ibid., 285–88, and "Articles of War," 229, 241.

35. Winthrop, *Military Law*, 448–58.

36. Ibid.

37. John Henry Wigmore, "Lessons from Military Justice," *Journal of the American Judicature Society* 4 (February 1921): 151. Emphasis in the original.

38. See testimony of Samuel T. Ansell in *Hearing Before a Subcommittee of the Committee of Military Affairs,* 66th Cong., 1st sess., 273–95; Brown, "Crowder-Ansell Dispute," 1–45; Frederic G. Bauer, "The Court-Martial Controversy and the New Articles of War," *Massachusetts Law Quarterly* 6 (February 1921): 61–86.

39. Samuel T. Ansell, "Military Justice," *Cornell Law Quarterly* 5 (November 1919): 1; Sherman, "The Civilianization of Military Law," 5–6.

40. Edmund M. Morgan, "The Existing Court-Martial System and the Ansell Army Articles," *Yale Law Journal* 29 (January 1919): 67.

41. Testimony of Colonel Frederick B. Wiener, in *Hearings on HR 2498 before a Subcommittee of the House Committee on Armed Forces*, 81st Cong., 1st sess. (1949), 781–83.

42. Sherman, "The Civilianization of Military Law," 7. See also Robert E. Quinn, "The Role of Criticism in the Development of Law," *Military Law Review* 35 (January 1967): 48, and *Manual for Courts-Martial United States (2005 Edition)*, Rules 201, 504, 912.

43. *Reid v. Covert*, 354 U.S. 1, 35–36 (1957). See also *United States ex rel. Toth v. Quarles*, 350 U.S. 11, 11–19 (1955).

44. *O'Callahan v. Parker*, 395 U.S. 266 (1969).

45. Joseph W. Bishop, Jr., *Justice Under Fire: A Study of Military Law*, 23–24.

46. John S. Cooke, "Introduction: Fiftieth Anniversary of the Uniform Code of Military Justice Symposium," *Military Law Review* 73 (September 2000): 3–4.

47. Hagan, "Introduction," in Winthrop, *Military Law*.

48. George S. Prugh, Jr., "Colonel William Winthrop: The Tradition of the Military Lawyer," *American Bar Association Journal* 42 (February 1956): 190–91.

49. See *Salim Ahmed Hamdan v. Donald H. Rumsfeld, Secretary of Defense et al.*, 548 U.S. 1–185 (2006), 33. Winthrop is cited at 25–26, 31, 33–34, 36, 40, 54, 61–62, and numerous other times.

50. "Articles of War, 1874," *Revised Statutes of the United States, 1873–74*, 229, 232.

51. Winthrop, *Military Law*, 534–36, 608.

52. Ibid., 577–86.

CHAPTER 4. COURT-MARTIAL

1. Testimony of Kid, "General Court-Martial of First Sergeant Kid, Company A, Indian Scouts," Records Received 4475, December 27, 1887, RG 153, NA, 1–3; William H. Powell, comp., *List of Officers of the Army of the United States from 1779 to 1900*, I, 176; and *Biographical Register of the Officers and Graduates of the U.S. Military Academy, Supplement*, vol. VI-A, 370.

2. "Articles of War, 1874," in *Revised Statutes of the United States, 1873–74*, 231.

3. See William A. Dobak and Thomas D. Phillips, *The Black Regulars, 1866–1898*, 184–92, 203–23.

4. William Winthrop, *Military Law and Precedents*, 291–92.

5. "General Court-Martial of First Sergeant Kid," 17–18.

6. Clare V. McKanna, Jr., *Race and Homicide in Nineteenth-Century California*, 1–31, and Clare V. McKanna, Jr., *White Justice in Arizona: Apache Murder Trials in the Nineteenth Century*.

7. "General Court-Martial of First Sergeant Kid," 27.

8. Powell, *List of Officers of the Army*, 708.

9. Ibid., 204, 365, 401, 574, 713, 905.

10. Baldwin's challenges, "General Court-Martial of First Sergeant Kid," 3–16.

11. Testimony of Captain Francis E. Pierce, ibid., 27.

12. Ibid., 37–39.

13. Ibid., 41–44.

14. Comments by Baldwin, ibid., 42, 44.

15. Testimony of Pierce, ibid., 46–47.

16. Ibid., 50–51.

17. Testimony of Al Sieber, ibid., 53.

18. Ibid., 53–59.

19. Comment by Baldwin, ibid., 60.

20. Testimony of Sieber, ibid., 58–62.

21. Testimony of Frederick Knipple, ibid., 63–65.

22. Testimony of Captain Alpheus Bowman, ibid., 66–67.

23. Ibid., 68–71.

24. Testimony of William Duchin, ibid., 73–75.

25. Ibid., 76–80.

26. Testimony of Charles S. Chew, ibid., 81–85.

27. Testimony of Tony, first sergeant, Indian Scouts, ibid., 87–88.

28. Testimony of Antonio Díaz, interpreter, ibid., 89.

29. Ibid.; Phyllis de la Garza, *The Apache Kid*; Dan Thrapp, *Al Sieber: Chief of Scouts*, 329–32.

30. Testimony of Díaz, "General Court-Martial of First Sergeant Kid," 90–92.

31. Ibid., 94.

32. Ibid., 96.

33. Testimony of Al Sieber, ibid., 98–104.

34. Testimony of Gonshayee, ibid., 105–7.

35. Testimony of Vacasheviejo, May 29, 1888, in *U.S. v. Gonshayee*, District Court, Second Judicial District, Arizona Territory, June 1888, NA, Laguna Niguel, CA, 14–16.

36. Testimony of Sayes, ibid., 109–14.

37. Enlistment of Kid, First Sergeant Scouts, in "Register of Enlistments in the U.S. Army, Indian Scouts, 1878–1914," NA.

38. Testimony of Kid, "General Court-Martial of First Sergeant Kid," 115–16.

39. Ibid., 116–17.

40. Ibid., 117–18.

41. Grenville Goodwin, *The Social Organization of the Western Apache*, 218.

42. Dorothy Bray, ed., *Western Apache–English Dictionary: A Community-Generated Bilingual Dictionary*, 377, 389, 400.

43. Ibid., 341, 359.

44. Summation of First Lieutenant John A. Baldwin, "General Court-Martial of First Sergeant Kid," 119–20.

45. Ibid., 118–21.

46. Ibid., 121–24.

47. Ibid., 125–26.

48. Ibid., 127–28.

49. Ibid., 128–30.

50. Ibid., 118.

51. Verdict and sentence, ibid., 130.

52. Robert Utley, *Frontier Regulars: The United States Army and the Indian, 1866–1891*, 80–87.

53. Britton Davis, *The Truth about Geronimo*; Charles B. Gatewood, *Lt. Charles Gatewood and His Apache Wars Memoir*.

54. Winthrop, *Military Law*, 639, 643–44.

55. Ibid., 644, and "Articles of War," 229.

56. Thrapp, *Al Sieber*, 329.

57. Winthrop, *Military Law*, 490.

58. William Gilmore Beymer, *On Hazardous Service: Scouts and Spies of the North and South*, 48–57.

CHAPTER 5. THE APPEALS

1. "Articles of War, 1874," in *Revised Statutes of the United States, 1873–74*, 239–40.

2. William Winthrop, *Military Law and Precedents*, 447–53, 475–78.

3. W. McKee Dunn, *A Sketch of the History and Duties of the Judge Advocate General's Department, U.S. Army, Washington, D.C., March 1, 1878*, 1–5.

4. William F. Fratcher, "History of the Judge Advocate General's Corps, United States Army," *Military Law Review* 4 (April 1959): 96.

5. Dunn, *Judge Advocate General's Department*, 10–12.

6. U.S. Army, Judge Advocate General's Corps, *The Army Lawyer: A History of the Judge Advocate General's Corps, 1775–1975*, 76–77.

7. Ibid., 79–86.

8. James Grant Wilson and John Fiske, eds., *Appletons' Cyclopaedia of American Biography*, 3:711.

9. Ibid.

10. Winthrop, *Military Law*, 53–54, 461.

11. Brian C. Pohanka, *Nelson A. Miles: A Documentary Biography of His Military Career, 1861–1903*, 147.

12. Nelson A. Miles, *Personal Recollections and Observations of General Nelson A. Miles*, 445; *Annual Report of Brigadier General Nelson A. Miles, Department of Arizona, 1887*, Appendix "A," 1.

13. *The Army Lawyer*, 76–79.

14. Sentence of the panel and final mitigation report of General Miles, "General Court-Martial of First Sergeant Kid," December 27, 1887.

15. General Miles, Orders to Major Anson Mills, Presiding Officer, Regarding Changes in Court-Martial of First Sergeant Kid, July 29, 1887, in "General Court-Martial of First Sergeant Kid," Appendix A, 1.

16. Ibid., 1–2.

17. Ibid., 2–3.

18. Ibid., 3–4.

19. John Godwin, *Alcatraz: 1868–1963*, 58, 71–73.

20. Davis, *Truth about Geronimo*, 130.

21. Clare V. McKanna, Jr., "Crime and Punishment: The Hispanic Experience in San Quentin, 1851–1880," *Southern California Quarterly* 72 (Spring 1990): 1–18.

22. "Articles of War, 1874," in *Revised Statutes*, 238; Winthrop, *Military Law*, 205–13.

23. Winthrop, *Military Law*, 217–24.

24. G. Norman Lieber, Acting Judge Advocate General, Appeals Report, to W. C. Endicott, Secretary of War, in "General Court-Martial of First Sergeant Kid," 4–5.

25. Ibid., 5–7.

26. Ibid., 7–9.

27. Ibid., 9–14.

28. Ibid., 14–17.

29. Ibid., 17–20.

30. Ibid., 20–24.

31. Ibid., 25–26.

32. Ibid., 28, 30–32.

33. Ibid., 43–44, 47.

34. John Tweedle, secretary for the War Department, to G. Norman Lieber, Acting Judge Advocate General, April 13, 1888, in Miscellaneous Documents Regarding Kid's General Court-Martial, Judge Advocate General, Records Received, 4475, RG 153, NA.

35. *U.S. Constitution*, Article III and Amendment V.

36. *Johnson v. Sayre*, 158 U.S. 109 (1895), 111–18.

37. *Reaves v. Ainsworth*, 219 U.S. 296 (1911), 304.

38. Correspondence by G. Norman Lieber, John Tweedle, and General O. O. Howard, October 13–29, 1888, in Miscellaneous Documents Regarding Kid's General Court-Martial.

39. Phyllis de la Garza, *The Apache Kid*, 64–65.

40. *Ex Parte Gonshayee* 130 U.S. 343–53 (1889).

41. Dan R. Williamson, "Apache Kid: Red Renegade of the West," *Arizona Highways* 15 (May 1939): 31.

42. Dan Thrapp, *Al Sieber: Chief of Scouts*, 327.

43. Winthrop, *Military Law*, 878.

44. Clare V. McKanna, Jr., "Murderers All: The Treatment of Indian Defendants in Arizona Territory, 1880–1912," *American Indian Quarterly* 17, no. 3 (1993): 359–69; *Territory of Arizona v. Kid*, Case No. 118, District Court, Second Judicial District, Gila County, October 25, 1889, Arizona State Archives, Phoenix.

45. Clare V. McKanna, Jr., *White Justice in Arizona: Apache Murder Trials in the Nineteenth Century*, 92–93, 178–79.

46. Comment made in a speech given in Washington, DC, October 22, 1883. Gorton Carruth and Eugene Ehrlich, *The Harper Book of American Quotes* (New York: Harper and Row, Publishers, 1988), 307.

47. Oliver Wendell Holmes, Jr., "Law in Science and Science in Law," *Harvard Law Review* XII (1899): 237–38.

48. Clifford Geertz, *Local Knowledge: Further Essays in Interpretive Anthropology*, 173.

49. See McKanna, *White Justice in Arizona*, 174, and Clare V. McKanna, Jr., *Race and Homicide in Nineteenth-Century California*, 99–100.

EPILOGUE: RENEGADE

1. *The Oxford English Dictionary*, XIII, 611–12; Andrew H. Fisher, "They Mean to Be Indians Always: The Origins of Columbia River Indian Identity, 1860–1885," *Western Historical Quarterly* 32 (Winter 2001): 468–92.

2. Message from A. McD. McCook, Brigadier General, Commanding, Headquarters Department of Arizona, and Captain Albert L. Myer, Acting Indian Agent, to the Commissioner of Indian Affairs, August 25, 1894, *Annual Report of the Commissioner of Indian Affairs to the Secretary of the Interior for the Year 1895* (Washington, DC: Government Printing Office, 1895), 112.

3. Enlistment of Massai, November 7, 1885, in "Registers of Enlistments in the U.S. Army, Indian Scouts, 1878–1914," RG 94, NA.

4. *Territory of Arizona v. Massai*, Case No. 122, District Court, Second Judicial District, Arizona Territory, October 26, 1889.

5. Marion P. Maus, "A Campaign Against the Apaches, 1885–1886," in Nelson A. Miles, *Personal Recollections and Observations of General Nelson A. Miles*, 450–71; Britton Davis, *The Truth about Geronimo*, 197; and John G. Bourke, *On the Border with Crook*, 471.

6. Sherry Robinson, *Apache Voices: Their Stories of Survival as Told to Eve Ball*, 96–97.

7. *New York Times*, June 4, 1896.

8. Captain John L. Bullis, Report on San Carlos Agency, *Annual Report of the Commissioner of Indian Affairs to the Secretary of the Interior for the Year 1890* (Washington, DC: Government Printing Office, 1890), 11.

9. Captain Lewis Johnson, Report on San Carlos Agency, *Annual Report of the Commissioner of Indian Affairs, 1892*, 220.

10. Letter from A. McD. McCook, General Commanding, Headquarters

Department of Arizona, to Captain L. Johnson, acting Indian agent, November 12, 1892, U.S. Army File 10, Arizona State Archives.

11. Captain Lewis Johnson, Report on San Carlos Agency, *Annual Report of the Commissioner of Indian Affairs, 1893,* 122.

12. *New York Times,* October 20, 1892.

13. Ibid.

14. Ibid., August 13, 1893.

15. Ibid., May 10, 1896.

16. See coverage in the *New York Times,* August 3, 1890; September 4, 1892; October 20 and November 20, 1892; August 13, 1893; and May 10, 1896.

17. H. B. Wharfield, "Footnotes to History: Apache Kid and the Record," *Journal of Arizona History* 6 (Spring 1965): 45–46.

18. Grenville Goodwin and Neil Goodwin, *The Apache Diaries: A Father-Son Journey,* 115, 245–47; see also Thrapp, *Al Sieber,* 348–50.

19. Dan R. Williamson, "The Apache Kid: Red Renegade of the West," *Arizona Highways* 15 (May 1939): 31.

20. Shelley Bowen Hatfield, *Chasing Shadows: Indians along the United States–Mexico Border, 1876–1911,* 11, 118–23.

21. Robinson, *Apache Voices,* 74, 80–81; Dan R. Williamson, "Al Sieber, Famous Scout of the Southwest," *Arizona Historical Review* 3 (January 1931): 69; McKanna, *White Justice in Arizona,* 167–83.

22. Robinson, *Apache Voices,* 74, 80–81.

23. Wharfield, "Footnotes to History," 46; Robinson, *Apache Voices,* 84.

24. Thrapp, *Al Sieber,* 320.

BIBLIOGRAPHY

GOVERNMENT DOCUMENTS

"Articles of War" in *Revised Statutes of the United States, 1873–74*, Title XIV, chap. 5. Washington, DC: Government Printing Office, 1875.

"Court-Martial of Sergeant No. 2 (alias Dead Shot), Sergeant No. 4 (alias Dandy Jim), and Corporal No. 8 (alias Skippy)," Records Received, 2821, November 30, 1881, Judge Advocate General (Army), RG 153, National Archives, Washington, DC.

Crook, George. *Annual Report of General George Crook, Commanding Officer, U.S. Army, Department of Arizona, September 27, 1883*. Microfilm 554, no. 5588, Western Americana, Frontier History of the Trans-Mississippi West, 1550–1900, Research Publications, New Haven, CT, 1975.

———. *Annual Report of General George Crook, Commanding Officer, U.S. Army, Department of Arizona, September 9, 1885*. Microfilm 554, no. 5588, Western Americana, Frontier History of the Trans-Mississippi West, 1550–1900, Research Publications, New Haven, CT, 1975.

———. *Report to the Adjutant General, Military Division of the Pacific, September 27, 1883*. San Francisco Presidio.

"General Court-Martial of First Sergeant Kid, Company A, Indian Scouts," Records Received, 4475, December 27, 1887, Judge Advocate General (Army), RG 153, National Archives, Washington, DC.

Miles, Nelson A. *Annual Report of Brigadier General Nelson A. Miles, U.S. Army, Commanding Department of Arizona, 1887*. Los Angeles: n.p., 1888.

———. "Orders to Major Anson Mills, Presiding Officer, Regarding Changes in Court-Martial of First Sergeant Kid," Appendix A, Records Received, 4475,

Judge Advocate General (Army), RG 153, December 27, 1887, National Archives, Washington, DC.

———. *Reports of General Nelson A. Miles, Renegade Indians, June 1887–May 1889, San Carlos Reservation*, Microforms, M 689, Roll 536, National Archives, Washington, DC.

The Military Laws of the United States. Washington, DC: Government Printing Office, 1901.

Miscellaneous Documents Regarding Kid's General Court-Martial and Punishment at Alcatraz, Appendixes A, B, C, and D, Records Received, 4475, December 27, 1887, Judge Advocate General (Army), RG 153, National Archives, Washington, DC.

"Petition to the General Court-Martial First Sergeant Kid from First Lieutenant John A. Baldwin," Appendix B, Records Received, 4475, December 27, 1887, Judge Advocate General (Army), RG 153, National Archives, Washington, D.C.

Title 28, Chapter 4, Government of Indian Country, Section 2144 and 2146, in *Revised Statutes of the United States, 1873–74.* Washington, DC: Government Printing Office, 1875.

U.S. Army, "Registers of Enlistments in the U.S. Army, Indian Scouts, 1878–1914," Records of the Adjutant General's Office, 1780–1917, RG 94, M 233, Roll 71, National Archives, Washington, DC.

———, Judge Advocate General's Corps. *The Army Lawyer: A History of the Judge Advocate General's Corps, 1775–1975.* Buffalo: William S. Hein & Co., 1993.

U.S. Bureau of Indian Affairs. *Annual Reports of the Commissioner of Indian Affairs to the Secretary of the Interior.* 1880, 1881, 1889–96. Washington, DC: Government Printing Office, 1880–81, 1889–96.

U.S. Congress. *Annals of the Congress of the United States,* 9th Cong., 1st sess., Vol. XV, January 2, 1806. Washington, DC: Gales and Seaton, 1852.

———. *Congressional Record,* 66th Cong., 1st sess., *Hearing before a Subcommittee of the Committee of Military Affairs.* Washington, DC: Government Printing Office, 1919.

———. *Congressional Record,* 81st Cong., 1st sess., *Hearings on HR 2498 before a Subcommittee of the House Committee on Armed Forces.* Washington, DC: Government Printing Office, 1949.

———. *Medal of Honor, 1863–1968.* Washington, DC: Government Printing Office, 1968.

U.S. Department of Defense. *Manual for Courts-Martial United States (2005 Edition).* Washington, DC: Government Printing Office, 2005.

U.S. War Department. *A Manual for Courts-Martial, Courts of Inquiry and of Other Procedure under Military Law.* Washington, DC: Government Printing Office, 1917.

———. "Report of the Acting Judge-Advocate-General to the Secretary of War," October 24, 1888, in *Report of the Secretary of War, 1888,* Vol II. Washington, DC: Government Printing Office, 1888.

COURT CASES

Ex Parte Captain Jack, 130 U.S. 354 (1889).

Ex Parte Crow Dog, 109 U.S. 556–72 (1883).

Ex Parte Gonshayee, 130 U.S. 344 (1889).

Territory of Arizona v. Kid, Hale, Sayes, and Pashtentah, Case No. 118, U.S. District Court, Second Judicial District, Gila County, Arizona Territory, October 19, 1889. Arizona State Archives, Phoenix.

Territory of Arizona v. Massai, Case No. 122, U.S. District Court, Second Judicial District, Gila County, Arizona Territory, October 26, 1889. Arizona State Archives, Phoenix.

U.S. v. Sayes, Case No. 153, District Court, Second Judicial District, Arizona Territory, June 1888. National Archives, Laguna Niguel, CA.

NEWSPAPERS

Arizona Champion (Flagstaff)

Arizona Silver Belt (Globe)

Arizona Weekly Citizen (Tucson)

Arizona Weekly Enterprise (Florence)

New York Times

SECONDARY SOURCES

Above and Beyond: A History of the Medal of Honor from the Civil War to Vietnam. Boston: Boston Publishing Company, 1985.

Ansell, Samuel T. "Military Justice," *Cornell Law Quarterly* 5 (November 1919): 1–17.

Army Lawyer: A History of the Judge Advocate General's Corps, 1775–1975. Buffalo: William S. Hein & Co., 1993.

Aycock, William B., and Seymour W. Wurfel. *Military Law Under the Uniform Code of Military Justice.* Westport: Greenwood Press, 1972.

Ball, Eve. *Indeh: An Apache Odyssey.* Provo, UT: Brigham Young University Press, 1980.

Bauer, Frederic Gilbert. "The Court-Martial Controversy and the New Articles of War," *Massachusetts Law Quarterly* 6 (February 1921): 61–85.

Beymer, William G. *On Hazardous Service: Scouts and Spies of the North and South.* New York: Harper & Brothers Publishers, 1912.

Biographical Register of the Officers and Graduates of the U.S. Military Academy, Supplement, vol. VI-A. Saginaw, MI: Seemann and Peters, Printers, 1920.

Bishop, Joseph W., Jr. *Justice Under Fire: A Study of Military Law.* New York: Charterhouse, 1974.

Bourke, John G. *On the Border with Crook.* Lincoln: University of Nebraska Press, 1971.

Boyer, L. Bruce. *Childhood and Folklore: A Psychoanalytic Study of Apache Personality.* New York: The Library of Psychological Anthropology, Publishers, 1979.

Braatz, Timothy. *Surviving Conquest: A History of the Yavapai Peoples.* Lincoln: University of Nebraska Press, 2003.

Brand, C. E. *Roman Military Law.* Austin: University of Texas Press, 1968.

Bray, Dorothy, ed. *Western Apache–English Dictionary: A Community-Generated Bilingual Dictionary.* Tempe, AZ: Bilingual Press, 1998.

Clum, Woodworth. *Apache Agent: The Story of John P. Clum.* Lincoln: University of Nebraska Press, 1978.

Collins, Charles. *Apache Nightmare: The Battle of Cibecue Creek.* Norman: University of Oklahoma Press, 1999.

Cruse, Thomas. *Apache Days and After*. Lincoln: University of Nebraska Press, 1987.

Davis, Britton. *The Truth about Geronimo*. Lincoln: University of Nebraska Press, 1976.

De la Garza, Phyllis. *The Apache Kid*. Tucson: Westernlore Press, 1995.

DeMontravel, Peter R. *A Hero to His Fighting Men: Nelson A. Miles, 1839–1925*. Kent, OH: Kent State University Press, 1998.

Dobak, William A., and Thomas D. Phillips. *The Black Regulars, 1866–1898*. Norman: University of Oklahoma Press, 2001.

Dunlay, Thomas W. *Wolves for the Blue Soldiers: Indian Scouts and Auxiliaries with the United States Army, 1860–90*. Lincoln: University of Nebraska Press, 1982.

Dunn, W. McKee. *A Sketch of the History and Duties of the Judge Advocate General's Department, U.S. Army, Washington, D.C., March 1, 1878*. Washington, DC: T. McGill, 1878.

Fisher, Andrew H. "They Mean to Be Indians Always: The Origins of Columbia River Indian Identity, 1860–1885," *Western Historical Quarterly* 32 (Winter 2001): 468–92.

Forrest, Earle R., and Edwin B. Hill. *Lone War Trail of Apache Kid*. Pasadena: Trail's End Publishing Company, 1949.

Gatewood, Charles B. *Lt. Charles Gatewood and His Apache Wars Memoir*. Lincoln: University of Nebraska Press, 2005.

Geertz, Clifford. *Local Knowledge: Further Essays in Interpretive Anthropology*. New York: Basic Books, 1983.

Getty, Harry T. *The San Carlos Indian Cattle Industry*. Tucson: University of Arizona Press, 1963.

Godwin, John. *Alcatraz: 1868–1963*. Garden City, NY: Doubleday & Company, 1963.

Goodwin, Grenville. *The Social Organization of the Western Apache*. Chicago: University of Chicago Press, 1942.

———. *Western Apache Raiding and Warfare*. Tucson: University of Arizona Press, 1971.

———, and Neil Goodwin. *The Apache Diaries: A Father-Son Journey*. Lincoln: University of Nebraska Press, 2000.

Hall, Kermit L. *The Magic Mirror: Law in American History*. New York: Oxford University Press, 1989.

Hansen, Donald W. "Judicial Functions of the Commander?" *Military Law Review* 41 (July 1968): 1–54.

Harring, Sidney L. *Crow Dog's Case: American Indian Sovereignty, Tribal Law, and United States Law in the Nineteenth Century.* Cambridge: Cambridge University Press, 1994.

Hatfield, Shelley Bowen. *Chasing Shadows: Indians along the United States–Mexico Border, 1876–1911.* Albuquerque: University of New Mexico Press, 1998.

Hayes, Jess G. *Apache Vengeance: True Story of Apache Kid.* Albuquerque: University of New Mexico Press, 1954.

Heitman, Francis. *Historical Register and Dictionary of the United States Army.* Washington, DC: Government Printing Office, 1903.

Hoebel, E. Adamson. *The Law of Primitive Man: A Study in Comparative Legal Dynamics.* Cambridge: Harvard University Press, 1954.

Holmes, Oliver Wendell, Jr. *The Common Law.* Boston: Little, Brown and Company, 1881.

Horn, Tom. *Life of Tom Horn: Government Scout and Interpreter.* Norman: University of Oklahoma Press, 1964.

Kearney, Thomas H., and Robert H. Peebles. *Arizona Flora.* Berkeley: University of California Press, 1960.

Kraft, Louis, ed. *Lt. Charles Gatewood and His Apache Wars Memoir.* Lincoln: University of Nebraska Press, 2005.

Laurie, Clayton D. "The Philippine Scouts: America's Colonial Army, 1899–1913," *Philippine Studies* 37 (Second Quarter 1989): 174–91.

Llewellyn, K. N., and E. Adamson Hoebel. *The Cheyenne Way: Conflict and Case Law in Primitive Jurisprudence.* Norman: University of Oklahoma Press, 1941.

Lockwood, Frank C. *More Arizona Characters.* Tucson: University of Arizona Press, 1943.

McCoy, Alfred W. "The Colonial Origins of Philippine Military Traditions," in *The Philippine Revolution of 1896: Ordinary Lives in Extraordinary Times,* ed. Florentino Rodao and Felice Noelle Rodríguez. Manila: Ateneo de Manila University Press, 2001.

McKanna, Clare V., Jr. "Crime and Punishment: The Hispanic Experience in San Quentin, 1851–1880," *Southern California Quarterly* 72 (Spring 1990): 1–18.

———. *Race and Homicide in Nineteenth-Century California.* Reno: University of Nevada Press, 2003.

————. *White Justice in Arizona: Apache Murder Trials in the Nineteenth Century.* Lubbock: Texas Tech University Press, 2005.

McKee, W. Dunn. *A Sketch of the History and Duties of the Judge Advocate Generals Department.* Washington, DC: T. McGill, 1878.

Miles, Nelson A. *Personal Recollections and Observations of General Nelson A. Miles.* Chicago: The Werner Company, 1896.

Morgan, Edmund M. "The Existing Court-Martial System and the Ansell Army Articles," *Yale Law Journal* 29 (1919): 52–74.

Opler, Morris. *An Apache Life-Way: The Economic, Social, and Religious Institutions of the Chiricahua Indians.* Lincoln: University of Nebraska Press, 1996.

Pohanka, Brian C. *Nelson A. Miles: A Documentary Biography of His Military Career, 1861–1903.* Glendale, CA: The Arthur H. Clark Company, 1985.

Powell, Michael A. "Crow Dog and the Issue of Tribal Jurisdiction," in *Law in the Western United States,* ed. Gordon Morris Bakken. Norman: University of Oklahoma Press, 2000.

Powell, William H. *List of Officers of the Army of the United States from 1779 to 1900.* Detroit: Gale Research Company, 1967.

Reagan, Albert B. *Notes on the Indians of the Fort Apache Region.* New York: American Museum of Natural History, 1930.

Robinson, Charles M., III, ed. *The Diaries of John Gregory Bourke,* Vol. 1, *November 20, 1872–July 28, 1876.* Denton: University of North Texas Press, 2003.

————. *General Crook and the Western Frontier.* Norman: University of Oklahoma Press, 2001.

Robinson, Sherry. *Apache Voices: Their Stories of Survival as Told to Eve Ball.* Albuquerque: University of New Mexico Press, 2000.

Schultz, Fred L. "An Apache Army Scout Turns Renegade," *American Illustrated History* 17, no. 4 (1982): 46–47.

Seagle, William. *The Quest for Law.* New York: Alfred A. Knopf, 1941.

Sherman, Edward F. "The Civilianization of Military Law," *Maine Law Review* 22 (January 1970): 3–169.

Smith, Sherry L. *The View from Officers' Row: Army Perception of Western Indians.* Tucson: University of Arizona Press, 1990.

Sonnichsen, C. L. "The Apache Kid," *Around Here, the Southwest in Pictures and Story* 10, no. 1 (1952): 61–62.

Sparks, William. *The Apache Kid: A Bear Fight and Other True Stories of the Old West.* Los Angeles: Skelton Publishing Company, 1926.

Ten Kate, Herman. *Travels and Researches.* Albuquerque: University of New Mexico Press, 2004.

Thrapp, Dan L. *Al Sieber: Chief of Scouts.* Norman: University of Oklahoma Press, 1964.

———. *General Crook and the Sierra Madre Adventure.* Norman: University of Oklahoma Press, 1972.

Utley, Robert M. *Frontier Regulars: The United States Army and the Indian, 1866–1891.* New York: Macmillan Publishing Co., 1973.

———. "The Ordeal of Plenty Horses," *American Heritage: The Magazine of History* 36 (December 1974).

Wharfield, H. B. *Apache Indian Scouts.* El Cajon, CA: n.p., 1964.

———. "Footnotes to History: Apache Kid and the Record," *Journal of Arizona History* 6 (Spring 1965): 37–46.

———. *10th Cavalry and Border Fights.* El Cajon, CA: n.p., 1965.

Williamson, Dan R. "Al Sieber, Famous Scout of the Southwest," *Arizona Historical Review* 3 (January 1931): 60–77.

———. "Apache Kid: Red Renegade of the West," *Arizona Highways* 15 (May 1939): 14–15, 30–31.

Winthrop, William. *Military Law and Precedents.* Boston: Little, Brown and Co., 1896; reprint, Buffalo: William Hein & Co., 2000.

Wilson, James Grant, and John Fiske, eds. *Appletons' Cyclopaedia of American Biography* 3. New York: D. Appleton and Company, 1898.

Wooster, Robert. *Nelson A. Miles and the Twilight of the Frontier Army.* Lincoln: University of Nebraska Press, 1993.

INDEX

Page numbers in *italics* indicate maps or photographs.